Best Hikes With
CHILDREN®
in Connecticut,
Massachusetts,
& Rhode Island

Best Hikes With
CH LDREN®
in Connecticut, Massachusetts, & Rhode Island

Cynthia C. Lewis
& Thomas J. Lewis

THE
MOUNTAINEERS

For Anya and Alexandra, our favorite hiking companions

The authors wish to thank Daniel and Cecelia Lewis and Sharlene and Clayton Copeland for the many babysitting assignments they cheerfully accepted while we finished the field work for this book. We also appreciate the efforts of Julie and Ellie White, who lent material and assistance.

First edition: first printing 1991, second printing 1992, third printing 1994, fourth printing 1996, fifth printing 1997

No part of this book may be reproduced in any form, or by any electronic, mechanical, or other means, without permission in writing from the publisher.

Published by The Mountaineers
1001 SW Klickitat Way, Suite 201, Seattle, Washington 98134

Published simultaneously in Canada by Douglas & McIntyre, Ltd., 1615 Venables Street, Vancouver, B.C. V5L 2H1

Published simultaneously in Great Britain by Cordee, 3a DeMontfort Street, Leicester, England, LE1 7HD

Manufactured in the United States of America

Edited by Lorretta Palagi
Maps by Newell Cartographics
Cover design by Elizabeth Watson
Book design and layout by Bridget Culligan
Cover photograph: Kent Falls in Kent, Connecticut; frontispiece: Shuffling through fall leaves on the way to Goat Peak in Massachusetts; page 24: Summer crowds at Sherwood Island, Connecticut; page 120: Pine Cobble summit, Massachusetts; page 212: Block Island, Rhode Island's Mohegan Bluffs
All photographs by Cynthia C. and Thomas J. Lewis

Library of Congress Cataloging in Publication Data
Lewis, Cynthia Copeland, 1960-
    Best hikes with children in Connecticut, Massachusetts, and Rhode Island / Cynthia C. Lewis and Thomas J. Lewis.
      p. cm.
    Includes index.
    ISBN 0-89886-265-5
    1. Hiking—New England—Guide-books. 2. Family recreation—New England—Guide-books. 3. New England—Description and travel—1981-—Guide-books. I. Lewis, Thomas J. (Thomas Joseph), 1958-
II. Title.
GV199.42.N38L48   1991
917.4'0443—dc20   90-28611
                               CIP

Contents

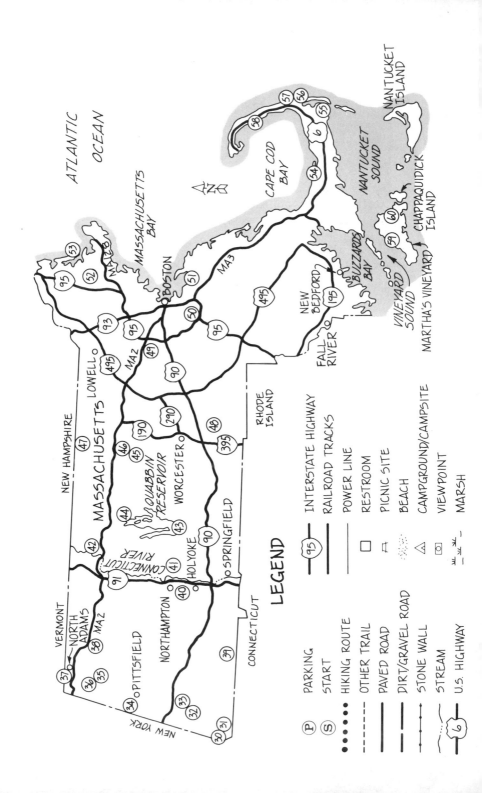

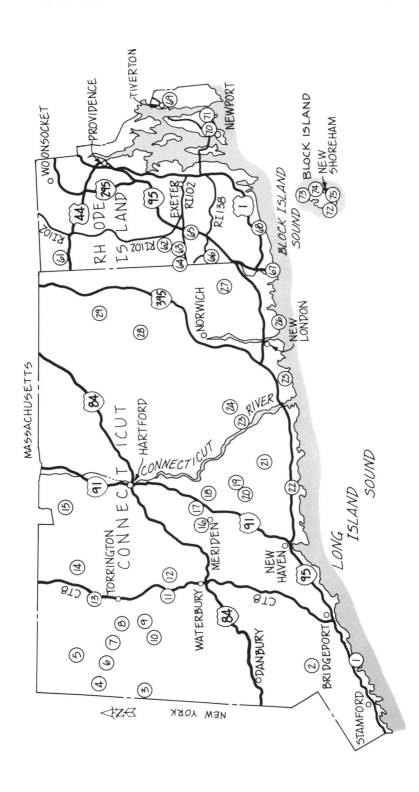

KEY TO SYMBOLS

 Dayhikes. These hikes can easily be completed in a day or part of a day. Camping along the trail is not recommended or is prohibited.

 Backpack trips. Overnight camping is permitted along the trail in designated areas (some with structures or facilities) or a public campground is within reasonable walking distance of the hiking trail. In every case, the campground or camping area appears on the accompanying map.

 Easy trails. These are relatively short, smooth, gentle trails suitable for small children or first-time hikers.

 Moderate trails. Most of these are 2 to 4 miles total distance and feature more than 500 feet of elevation gain. The trail may be rough and uneven. Hikers should wear lug-soled boots and be sure to carry the Ten Essentials (see below).

 Difficult trails. These are often rough, with considerable elevation gain or distance to travel. They are suitable for older or experienced children. Lug-soled boots and the Ten Essentials are standard equipment.

 Hikable. The best times of year to hike each trail are indicated by the following symbols: flower—spring; sun—summer; leaf—fall; snowflake—winter.

 Driving directions. These paragraphs tell you how to get to the trailheads.

 Turnarounds. These are places, mostly along moderate trails, where families can cut their hike short yet still have a satisfying outing. Turnarounds usually offer picnic opportunities, views, or special natural attractions.

 Cautions. These mark potential hazards—cliffs, stream or highway crossing, and the like—where close supervision of children is strongly recommended.

Introduction

It's only after we shell out $59.99 for the Intergalactic Supersonic Warriors TV video game that we realize little Frank would rather spend the afternoon outside, giving a rock family a bath in a puddle. Kids and the outdoors are a natural combination. And family hiking adds an element of adventure to the out-of-doors: What will we find around the next bend? A cave? A boardwalk? A waterfall maybe? The feeling of accomplishment shared by everyone after the final climb to the summit is especially valuable for the youngster who may not excel in football or long division. Hiking is within the capabilities of nearly every child and it builds self-confidence and heightens self-esteem. Also, it's fun for everyone—no one has to compromise. As a final bonus, it's one of the healthiest family activities around.

To be sure, there are potential complications in family hiking. Fatigue, sore feet, and bug bites may not be serious but will make a hike less enjoyable for the little tykes. Children become bored, hungry, and just plain cranky. Injuries, serious bites, contact with poisonous plants, getting lost, or finding yourself in the midst of a spring blizzard present more serious difficulties. Planning for the obvious (hunger) as well as for the less likely (an encounter with poison ivy) will reduce if not eliminate any problems. Because children seem to have excellent memories for the less-than-terrific times, adequate preparation is critical.

Hiking Tips

Here are a few pointers for hiking with young children.

- **Bring a little buddy.** A friend is a distraction from that blister on his big toe and a deterrent to whining: Nobody wants to look wimpy in front of a school chum!
- **Set a realistic pace.** A child's pace varies tremendously within the course of a walk, ranging from ambling along, examining every stone, leaf, and blade of grass to racing ahead like the lead runner in the Boston Marathon. By letting the child set the pace (within reason), you will convey the message that a hike's success is not measured in terms of miles covered but rather in the pleasure taken in each step along the way.

- **Choose an appropriate hike.** When in doubt, easier is better than harder, but an athletic twelve-year-old will be bored with the mile-long amble through the woods that is better suited for a preschooler.
- **Give compliments.** Nothing means more to a child than a parent patting him or her on the back and saying that he or she is the best climber around. Such praise makes sore feet suddenly feel a whole lot better.
- **Make frequent stops.** A trailside boulder, fallen tree, breezy peninsula.... Children may need more frequent rests than adults, but they tend to recover more quickly. Teach them to pace themselves; remind them as they dash out of the car that it will be a long climb to the summit.
- **Offer snacks.** Granola bars, bananas, cheese cubes, a mixture of nuts, chocolate chips, and dried fruits, boxes of raisins—bring along any favorite that will boost energy. Bring plenty of water, too.
- **Play games on the trail.** Have in mind things for children to listen and look for—croaking frogs, deer tracks, birds flying south for the winter. Collect acorns, autumn leaves, or pretty stones. Offer incentives and distractions—"we're halfway there," "the waterfall is just over the hill"—and talk about the day's goals. Have fun—laughter lightens the load for everyone.
- **Encourage responsibility.** Children, like the rest of us, tend to meet the level of expectation. An older child given the responsibility of following the hike on the map, keeping an eye out for a loon through the binoculars, or charting directions with the compass will proudly fulfill his or her duties and be less likely to engage in horseplay.
- **Maintain a good attitude.** Misery is contagious, so even if you are anxious because you think it might rain or your pack has somehow doubled its weight in the last half-mile, don't complain in front of your kids. A bad attitude will kill a good time much faster than a pair of soggy sneakers.

Hiking Etiquette

Sometimes the very qualities that make children so much fun to have along on a hike can present the most problems. Adults recognize that what our ancestors referred to as "dismal wilderness" is our most valuable and threatened resource, but to children the outdoors is a vast playground. While the seven-year-old is gleefully stripping a boulder of its moss blanket in search of worms and beetles, his younger sister is stomping among the wildflowers reciting a spontaneous ode to posies. But by springing to the defense of each cluster of ferns parents may be concerned that they will turn what should be a relaxed family outing into a battle. How can parents creatively direct their children's enthusiasm toward nature-friendly pursuits?

Older children can anticipate the consequences of their own actions on the environment. They will learn respect for the wilderness and its inhabitants from their parents' examples. By recycling, buying biodegradable products, and supporting environmental concerns, parents integrate a conservation ethic into the family's daily life so that "clean hiking" and "clean camping" come naturally to their children. Youngsters so raised understand that as hikers and campers they are becoming, for a time, part of the wilderness; they are not seeking to dominate or ruin it. Willingly, they'll "take nothing but pictures, leave nothing but footprints, and kill nothing but time." Children old enough to distinguish "safe" from potentially harmful trash can be encouraged to pick up the litter of previous hikers as well.

Younger children are more likely than older ones to act recklessly and without concern for the environment and its inhabitants. Offering desirable options rather than simply forbidding certain behavior works best with most children. Instead of picking a wildflower, your daughter can smell it, examine the petals under a magnifying glass, or take a photograph. Binoculars, as well, focus attention on soaring birds or far horizons. Such equipment retains its appeal when it is reserved just for special outings. One of the greatest gifts we can give our children is to instill in them a respect for the other living things that share our planet and an understanding of their own importance in determining the future of our natural environment.

Here are some specific ways that hikers can leave the forest without a trace:

- Prepare to take trash out with you by bringing along appropriate bags or containers.
- Stick to the trails and, when presented with the choice of stepping on delicate vegetation or rocks, pick the rocks.
- Trails are most vulnerable during "mud season" in March and April; be especially careful then.

- Don't wash directly in streams or lakes.
- If rest room facilities are not provided, dig a small hole for human waste far from any water source and cover it with soil afterward.
- Conform to the specific regulations of the state park, wildlife refuge, or other recreation area you are visiting.

Safety

While you cannot completely eliminate the risks inherent in hiking mountain or forest trails, you can minimize them by taking proper precautions and by educating yourself and your children. To help combat the most frequent problems, you should carry the "Ten Essentials" listed on page 16, such as a well-equipped first-aid kit, flashlight, map, and extra food and clothing. Recognize your own limitations and those of your children: Don't attempt to climb Mount Algo (Connecticut's longest, steepest climb) on your first family outing. If you're hiking with very young children, you will probably wind up carrying them or at least their packs for some of the way, so choose a hike that is well within your own capabilities.

Getting Lost

Although we have described as accurately as possible the trail conditions and routes, conditions may be different when you embark on a given hike. Blazes may be painted over or seasonal changes, such as erosion or fallen trees, may cause a trail to be rerouted or bridges and boardwalks to collapse. You may want to change your plans if the trail seems too poorly marked to follow or if the condition of the trail is dangerous.

Prepare for the possibility of getting lost. Leave your itinerary with a friend or relative (or at the very least, leave a visible note on the dashboard of the car). Carry enough extra food and clothing so that if an overnight is necessary, you are prepared.

Teach your older kids to read maps and all of them to pay close attention to trail markers. On most marked trails, they should be able to see two blazes (one ahead of them and one behind them) at all times. They need to know that double blazes indicate a significant change of direction and triple blazes usually signal the end of the trail. You may want to equip everyone with a whistle and establish a whistle code or insist on the buddy system. Encourage children to stay put as soon as they realize they are lost. Above all, emphasize the importance of alertness and remaining calm. If you are unable to attempt a return to your car because you are lost or injured or both, make a fire using greens that will smoke and signal anyone looking.

Weather

Be conscious of weather conditions and do not hesitate to rechart your course due to a potential storm. Even the least challenging trail can pose a hazard in foul weather. The only thing worse than getting caught in a severe thunderstorm or blizzard while hiking is getting caught in such a storm while hiking with your children.

If children are particulary engrossed in what they are doing, they may ignore discomfort or an injury. (Remember how they swim in a lake for hours until they have blue lips and are covered with goosebumps, coming ashore only at your insistence?) Watch for signs of fatigue—encourage a rest and food stop. Remember, too, that certain conditions, such as hypothermia, may affect a child sooner than an adult exposed to the same climate. If a child seems listless and cranky (early signs of hypothermia), and certainly once he complains of being cold or begins shivering, add another layer of warm clothes or offer hot chocolate or soup.

Water

Hikers need to drink frequently and the best way to ensure a safe water supply is to bring it along. It's never a good idea to drink water from an unknown source. If you must, boil it first (for at least 10 to 15 minutes, including cooking water) or use a filter designed to remove *Giardia lamblia,* a microscopic parasite.

Ticks

Lyme Disease has attracted a lot of attention lately. The deer ticks that spread the disease are known to inhabit much of the area covered by this guide, most notably the coastal sections. Although in its later stages Lyme Disease can lead to arthritis and heart and neurological problems, if detected early it can be effectively treated with antibiotics. A red, ringlike rash at the site of the bite is the most common first symptom, often followed by a flulike fever, fatigue, a headache, and stiff, sore joints. As important as recognizing early symptoms, however, is knowing how to prevent the disease. When hiking in places known to harbor deer ticks, wear light-colored clothing because the ticks are easier to see on light colors. Opt for a long-sleeved shirt with snug collar

Cape Cod's Seaside Trail is ideal for pint-size beachcombers.

and cuffs and tuck long pants into high socks. After the hike, check yourself and your children for the tiny ticks. If you remove a tick with tweezers within 24 hours, the disease is usually not transmitted, and not all deer ticks carry the disease.

Dogs

Dogs can also present a danger to your kids. Locals often use trails to exercise unleashed pets. While the kids probably won't get bitten or attacked, they may get knocked over or frightened by an unexpected encounter with a German shepherd. On trails that allow dogs, you may want to stay close to small children.

The Ten Essentials

The Mountaineers recommends ten items that should be taken on every hike, whether a day trip or an overnight. When children are involved and you are particularly intent on making the trip as trouble-free as possible, these "Ten Essentials" may avert disaster.

1. Extra clothing. It may shower, the temperature may drop, or wading may be too tempting to pass up. Be sure to include rain gear, extra shoes and socks (especially a pair of shoes that can be used for wading when bare feet might mean sliced toes), a warm sweater, and hat and mittens.

2. Extra food. Too much is better than not enough. Carry sufficient water in canteens or fanny packs in case no suitable source is available on the trail.

3. Sunglasses. Look for a pair that screens UV rays.

4. Knife. Chances are you will never need it, but if you do and it's with the string and masking tape in the top drawer to the left of the refrigerator, you'll be sorry.

5. Firestarter—candle or chemical fuel. If you must build a fire, these are indispensable.

6. First-aid kit. Don't forget to include moleskin for blisters, baking soda to apply to stings, and any special medication your child might need if he or she is allergic to bee stings or other insect bites.

7. Matches in a waterproof container. You can buy these matches in a store that carries hiking and camping gear.

8. Flashlight. Check the batteries before you begin your hike.

9. Map. Don't assume you'll just "feel" your way to the summit.

10. Compass. Teach your children how to use it, too.

In addition to the Ten Essentials, a few other items can come in mighty handy, especially when young children are along.

Until you've hiked or camped during black fly season, it's hard to describe how immensely annoying a swarm of these little buggers can be. Insect repellent doesn't deter them all, but it helps. (Be sure the repellent you have is appropriate for children.) In addition to this protection, dress children in lightweight long-sleeved shirts and pants. A cap may come in handy as well. A head cover made of mosquito netting (with elastic to gather it at the neck or waist) may be a hike-saver, especially during spring hikes. And don't forget to protect children from the sun. Kids can get sunburned even in wintertime.

Binoculars, a camera, a magnifying glass, and a bag for collecting treasures are fun to have along and might keep children from trying to push each other into the brook.

Leave your poodle, portable radio, and noisy toys at home.

Equipment

Footgear

In selecting footgear, make comfort the number one priority. You do not want to find out two miles from the car that Mikey's boots (which were a tad small in the store but were half price) have turned his toes purple. Buying shoes that are too small, in fact, is probably the most common mistake new hikers make. Many stores specializing in outdoor equipment have steep ramps that you can stand on to simulate a downhill hike. If your toes press against the tip of the boot when you are standing on the ramp, try a larger size. When buying boots, be sure to bring the liners and socks that you plan to wear on hikes for a more accurate fit. (In most cases, the sales people in sporting goods stores are very helpful and will be able to guide you to an appropriate pair of boots.) You probably want lightweight, ankle-high, leather, or fabric and leather, boots. In a few cases, sneakers or running shoes will be adequate but, on most trails, hiking boots are preferrable. If you will be doing a lot of hiking, invest in a good pair that will hold up to rugged terrain. (Be sure to wear new boots at home for several days before hitting the trails.)

In the wintertime, insulated boots are a must, and in the spring or after a rainstorm, opt for waterproof boots. Snowshoes or cross-country skis can also be used for winter hikes on fairly level terrain, although I do not recommend winter hiking for children because it's not nearly as enjoyable for most kids as hiking in spring, summer, or fall.

Clothing

As with footgear, comfort is top priority. Think layers—they can be added or taken off as the temperature allows. Often, if you will be visiting a ravine or heading to a summit, factors such as wind and temperature will change noticeably. With layers, the moment you begin to feel warm you can remove an article of clothing to avoid becoming wet. In bug season long sleeves paired with long pants are best. Jeans, a perennial favorite among kids, aren't necessarily the most comfortable walking pants. When wet they are very heavy and cold, seem to take forever to dry, and unless well worn can be stiff as cardboard. A better bet might be sweatpants or cotton slacks or tights.

If hiking in cool weather, consider the new synthetic thermal long underwear. Cotton tends to retain moisture, whereas polypropylene keeps it away from your skin. You don't want to perspire on your climb and then become chilled once you stop for a

Young hikers admire a waterfall in Kent, Connecticut.

rest or head back to the car. Socks should be wool; try the rag-knit type found in most shoe or sporting goods stores. Wear a thin, silken liner under the socks. (Thick over thin will usually prevent blisters.) Hats will help keep the sun out of your eyes and the black flies out of your hair, and your head will be somewhat protected if a rain shower takes you by surprise.

A rain poncho with a hood that can be folded up into a small pack is essential for every member of the family.

Packs

Older children will probably want to carry their own packs, while the little ones will want to move unencumbered. Child-size packs can be purchased at stores carrying hiking and camping supplies—be aware, though, that they may quickly become too small. Unless you have a number of other little hikers who will be using it, you may want to just fill an adult pack with a light load. Kids like to carry their own liquids and snacks.

Adults should carry as light a load as possible because inevitably there will be times when a child needs or wants to be carried. Backpacks should have a lightweight but sturdy frame, fit comfortably, and have a waist belt to distribute the load.

Child-Related Equipment

Infants can be carried easily in front packs. We took our oldest daughter for a hike up Blue Hill in Massachusetts when she was just three weeks old. The walking rhythm and closeness to a parent is comforting to the littlest tykes. Older babies and toddlers do well in backpacks. They enjoy gazing around from a high vantage point and are easily carried by an adult. Look for a backpack that also has a large pouch for carrying other hiking essentials. We have also used a carrier resembling a hip sling that will accommodate children up to four years old. Ours folds into a wallet-sized pouch and can be put on when your three-year-old has had enough walking for the day. Look for ideas in outdoor stores, toy stores, and stores specializing in baby furniture and supplies. Ask hiking friends what they have found useful and, whenever possible, try before you buy.

Some of our hikes (Rhode Island's Cliff Walk, for instance) include sections with paved or hard-packed surfaces. For these hikes, a young child can be pushed in a stroller (bigger wheels make for easier pushing). However, none of our hikes are entirely on pavement, so you are probably better off finding some way of packing them.

Additional Equipment For Overnights

You will need additional equipment if you plan to spend the night on the trail. Sleeping bags, foam pads, a small stove and cooking utensils as well as a tent are obvious necessities. Generally, folks who work at stores stocking outdoor supplies are more than willing to help you outfit your family for an overnighter. In some cases, trailside shelters, tent platforms, or lean-tos will be available. Learn everything about the accommodations (including whether you need to reserve space) before your trip.

FOOD

If you are staying overnight, you may want to buy freeze-dried food, although the kids might prefer more familiar nourishment. While a food's nutritional value, weight, and ease of preparation should take precedence over taste, kids—even hungry ones—may turn up their nose at something that just doesn't taste right. You can try one-pot meals such as chili or beef stew or bring foods that require no cooking at all. Cooking equipment is cumbersome and it usually takes more time than you expect to prepare and cook the meal.

Dayhikers need easy-to-carry, high-energy snack foods. Forget about three, filling meals and eat light snacks as often as you are hungry. The time of year will affect your choices: You won't want to be peeling an orange with fingers frozen by the cold—you're better off with meatballs. Fruit that is not soft and easily squished is good—try dried fruit, raisins, papaya sticks, and banana chips. Fig bars, cheese cubes, granola, and nuts are also hiking favorites. Let the kids help you mix chocolate chips, peanuts, raisins, and other "gorp" ingredients since it's cheaper than buying the ready-made trail mix. My kids like granola bars—store-bought or homemade. Often, we buy a loaf of our favorite bakery bread and a hunk of mild cheese that will appeal to the kids and then hard boil some eggs to take with us. Let your family's taste buds and your good judgment determine what you take along.

My kids love these homemade energy bars (let yours help you make them):

¾ cup firmly packed brown sugar
½ cup honey
1½ cups chunky peanut butter
5 cups raisin bran cereal
6 ounces mixed dried fruit pieces

Grease a medium-sized baking pan and set aside. Stir the brown sugar and honey together in a saucepan. Bring the mixture to a boil, stirring continuously. Remove the brown sugar and honey from the heat and add the peanut butter. Stir until smooth. Add the cereal; mix well. Set aside ⅓ cup of the dried fruit pieces and add the rest to the peanut butter mixture. Spread the peanut butter mixture evenly in the prepared pan and top with the remaining fruit bits, pressing down firmly. After the mixture has cooled, cut it into bars and wrap each individually. (You can experiment by adding peanuts, chocolate chips, or any family favorite.)

How to Use This Book

This, the first of a two-volume series, covers southern New England: Connecticut, Massachusetts, and Rhode Island. The guide is divided into three sections by state, with a map for each that shows the locations of the hikes.

Selecting a Hike

Read the trip description thoroughly before selecting a hike. Each entry includes enough information for you to make a good choice.

Name: This is the name of the mountain, lake, or park as it will appear on most road maps.

Number: Use this to locate the hike on the state map.

Type: There are two possible choices for each entry. A "dayhike" means that this hike can easily be completed in a day or part of a day for most families. Camping overnight on the trail is prohibited. "Dayhike or overnight" refers to trails on which there are camping spots, lean-tos, shelters, or some place for you to stay overnight. Or, it may mean that a campground located within the recreation area that you are visiting is within reasonable walking distance of the hiking route. In either case, the overnight location is evident on the trail map. This indication does *not* mean that the hike is too long or difficult to be completed in an afternoon.

Difficulty: Hikes are rated easy, moderate, or difficult for children. Ratings are approximate, taking into consideration the length of the trip, elevation gains, and trail conditions. Don't reject a hike based on a difficult rating before noting the turnaround point or reading about an optional shortcut—the first section of trail might be perfect for little guys.

Distance: This is the *hiking* distance. If a side trip to a waterfall or view is included in the text and on the map, it is in the total distance. A part of the hike described within parentheses—whether a longer or a shorter route—is not factored into the total distance.

Hiking Time: Again, this is an estimate based on hiking length, elevation gains, and trail conditions that will vary somewhat from family to family. Short rest stops are factored in—longer lunch stops are not.

High Point: The number given reflects the height above sea level of the highest point on the trail.

Elevation Gain: Elevation gain indicates the total number of vertical feet gained during the course of the hike. When analyzing a hike, this notation will be more significant than the high point in determining difficulty.

Hikable: Based on such varied criteria as crowds, mosquito season, mud season, prefered hiking conditions, extra features along the trail (a swimming hole or view of the hawk migration), hunting season (when applicable), we have recommended months for you to hike the trails.

Maps: The name of the topographic map published by U. S. Geological Survey (USGS) is included for your reference. The contour lines offer a good indication of terrain features and are a good supplement to the maps in this guide. Be aware, however, that the trails may have changed since the map was printed, so don't necessarily follow them exclusively.

Each entry is divided into three general sections: a summary or history of the hike and region, driving and parking instructions, and a complete description of the hike. The symbols within the text, in the margins, and on the maps indicate turnaround points, views, campsites, drinking water, picnic spots, and caution. (See "Key to Symbols" on page 9.)

In some cases, a fee is charged for entry or parking. These fees are generally minimal (between $1 and $5) and some, such as those for Audubon properties, do not apply to members. Be aware that fees increase and some places that only charged in-season or didn't charge at all when we did our research may have changed their policies. It's best to come prepared with some cash.

A Word About Camping...

Vandalism and overuse of the trails has led to some strict regulations regarding backpack camping. Massachusetts allows wilderness camping only in those areas designated with signs as camping areas. Along the Appalachian Trail, camping is permitted in the Appalachian Trail shelters, designated campsites, and dispersed camping zones (also indicated by signs). If you would like more specific information, a copy of all Massachusetts regulations governing forests and parks is available from the Department of Environmental Management (see the list at the back of this book for mailing address). In Connecticut, camping along the trails in undesignated spots is prohibited. Some backpack camping sites have been created in association with the Connecticut Blue Trail system and the Appalachian Trail. These offer rustic (if any) facilities. In some spots, shelters have been erected; here, the stay is limited to one night. In Rhode Island, overnight camping in rest or picnic areas, in noncamping state or municipal parks, or on beaches is prohibited. Check with local police or conservation officers if there is a question as to the legality of an overnight stay. Camping areas are mentioned within a hike entry when they are operated by the same group that maintains the trail.

Happy hiking!

A Note About Safety

Safety is an important concern in all outdoor activities. No guidebook can alert you to every hazard or anticipate the limitations of every reader. Therefore, the descriptions of roads, trails, routes, and natural features in this book are not representations that a particular place or excursion will be safe for your party. When you follow any of the routes described in this book, you assume responsibility for your own safety. Under normal conditions, such excursions require the usual attention to traffic, road and trail conditions, weather, terrain, the capabilities of your party, and other factors. Keeping informed on current conditions and exercising common sense are the keys to a safe, enjoyable outing.

The Mountaineers

CONNECTICUT

---

1. Sherwood Island

Type:	Dayhike
Difficulty:	Easy for children
Distance:	2.7 miles, round trip
Hiking time:	2 hours
High point/elevation gain:	10 feet, 10 feet
Hikable:	Year-round
Maps:	USGS Sherwood Point

Sherwood Island State Park in Westport has the honor of being the first state park in Connecticut and one of the first in the United States. Does the name Sherwood Forest ring a bell with any of the little folks in the back seat? The park is named for the Sherwood family that moved here in the 1600s from England's Sherwood Forest—the same Sherwood Forest inhabited by Robin Hood and his band of merry men. Sherwood Island's 234 acres include marsh areas, wooded terrain, and more than a mile of beachfront. If you visit the island in the winter, you will probably have this stretch of beach to yourself. The children can bring along bird guidebooks and binoculars and try to identify sea birds

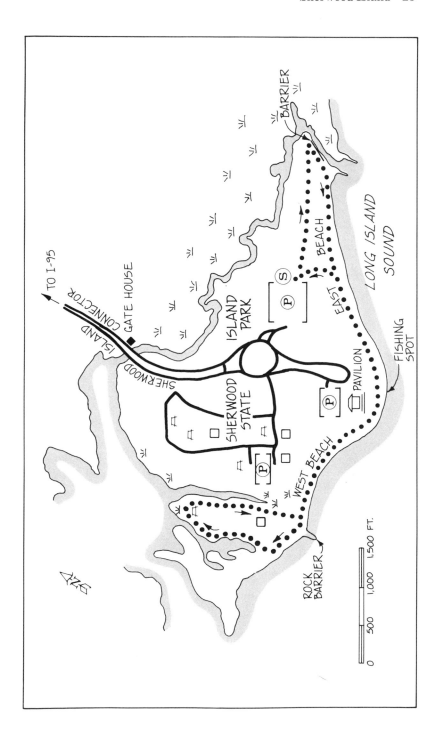

Look what I caught!

and other feathered fellows that have decided to brave the New England winter.

From the Connecticut Turnpike (I-95) in Westport, take Exit 18 (Sherwood Island) and turn south onto the Sherwood Island Connector. In 0.6 mile, you arrive at the gatehouse. (Pay a daily fee in season.) Drive to the easternmost parking lot.

Begin by walking along the grassy road heading toward the far eastern end of the park's beach (marked by a tidal stream bordered with flat boulders and a wooden barrier). The barrier makes a good balance beam for kids to test their skills. From here, travel west along the water's edge on a sandy beach. If you visit during low tide, watch for the birds that flock to the area to feed on trapped fish. Soon, the windswept beach surrenders to a rocky point that juts into Long Island Sound, a favorite spot for local fishermen. Shore fishermen are particularly numerous in autumn, when striped bass, flounder, and bluefish are active in the shallow waters near the beach. Beyond this section, the sandy beach returns. Ask the kids about ocean smells: What does seaweed smell like? Continue walking toward the westernmost end of the beach. At the rock barrier, sit and enjoy lunch or a snack. Turn right (north) at the far end of Sherwood Island and travel away from the beach onto a wooded, grassy knoll. Even when the island is crowded with sunbathers in the summer, this section of the island attracts few people. This peninsula, which extends into the inland salt marshes, is an ideal spot for bird-watching. Follow along the perimeter of the peninsula into the marsh at low tide. When you are ready, return to the beach and follow it back to your car.

Notes: There is a moderate in-season fee per car. Parking is free from Columbus Day to Memorial Day.

2. Devil's Den Preserve

Type: Dayhike
Difficulty: Moderate for children
Distance: 5.6 miles, loop
Hiking time: 4 hours
High point/elevation gain: 510 feet, 300 feet
Hikable: April–November
Maps: USGS Norwalk North

This 1,540-acre property, maintained by the Nature Conservancy, is the largest nature preserve in southwestern Connecticut. The 15 miles of well-maintained and easy-to-follow trails make this a great place for a family that is physically up to a longer hike, but doesn't have a great deal of hiking experience. You will sign in and out at the map shelter; the staff will check to see that all hikers have returned before nightfall. This preserve with its prehistoric Indian shelter cave, man-made lake and mill site, charcoal-manufacturing display, and meandering stone walls offers kids an interesting look at how humankind has affected and been affected by the natural world.

    Take Exit 42 off of CT-15 (Merritt Parkway). Travel north on CT-57 for about 3 miles to Weston center. At the northern junction of CT-57 and CT-53 in Weston, travel 1.6 miles north on CT-53 and turn left (west) on Godfrey Road. In 0.5 mile, turn right on Pent Road at the sign for the Nature Conservancy, Devil's Den Preserve. In 0.4 mile, the road ends at the parking area.

From the right-hand (east) side of the parking lot, locate the Laurel Trail and signs to Godfrey Pond. (Register here and pick up a trail map.) The yellow-blazed Laurel Trail is wide and carpeted with wood chips. Soon, you pass a recreation of a charcoal-manufacturing site. Parents can explain that charcoal is partially combusted wood. In the early 1800s, charcoal production was a major industry here. Most of the land was bare because the trees were constantly being cut to make charcoal. The trail continues, wandering through quiet woods and leading through breaks in stone walls. Tell the kids about farmers long ago who built stone walls to rid planted fields of rocks and keep farm animals penned in. No bulldozers or backhoes helped these hardy souls.

Family crossing a footbridge on the edge of Godfrey Pond

When you arrive at junction 22 (the number is found on top of telephone pole stumps as the path divides), bear right, still on the manicured path. Shortly, at junction 23, turn left and cross over a stream on a footbridge. At junction 24 (25 on the preserve's trail map), turn right. After a brief ascent followed by an equivalent descent, you will arrive at Godfrey Pond. This man-made lake was created to provide power for a sawmill that operated in the late 1700s and early 1800s. At the southern outlet to the pond is a small waterfall and the site of the old mill. This is an interesting area for kids to explore.

Cross the dam and turn left at junction 33 to follow along the eastern edge of the pond. At first, this red-blazed jeep path travels some distance from the pond. But when you follow the yellow trail that departs from the jeep path at junction 34, you descend to pond's edge. The trail curves around the pond over rocky terrain, crossing two streams on footbridges and sweeping along the west-

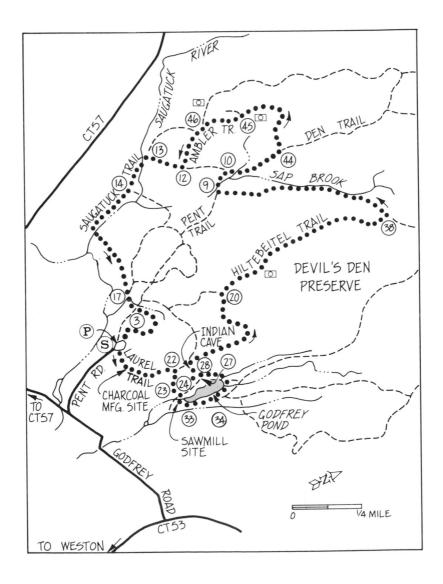

ern side of the pond. At junction 27, swing right onto Harrison Trail. Soon you arrive at an impressive rock overhang. As long ago as 5000 B.C., this cave served as a shelter for Indians who roamed the area to hunt, fish, and gather. Can the kids imagine what life must have been like for these prehistoric wanderers?

Junction 28 marks about 1 mile of hiking. Here, you can turn left and then right at junction 22 to return to your car via the Laurel Trail for a total hike of 1.5 miles; or you can continue by turning right at number 28 onto Cub Scout Trail. Maintained by a local scout troop, this narrow path winds through the hilly terrain, passing through a swamp over a unique log bridge. In a clearing at junction 20, 1.75 miles from the start, turn right onto the Hiltebeitel Trail. Don't be surprised if your footsteps urge a ruffed grouse out of the underbrush, startling the kids with its noisy flapping wings. Soon, you climb to a lookout at Deer Knoll (485 feet above sea level) with westerly vistas to Long Island Sound. You may be able to catch a glimpse of migrating hawks from here.

The trail continues over rock outcroppings and through dense woodlands, arriving at junction 38 at 2.5 miles. Turn left. This trail follows along Sap Brook and jumps across the stream several times before emerging at trail intersection 9, 3.25 miles from the start. Here, turn right onto the wide Pent Trail and soon bear right at junction 10, now on the Den Trail. Cross Sap Brook and in 300 yards at marker 44, turn left onto the narrow path called Ambler Trail. At the 4-mile mark, after an ascent, you arrive at a vista looking west over Ambler Gorge. To head back to the parking area from the Ambler Trail, bear left at junctions 45 and 46 and turn right at number 12 onto a wide cross-country ski trail. At junction 13, 4.5 miles from the start of the hike, turn left onto Saugatuck Trail and continue straight through junctions 14, 17, and 3 to the parking lot and your car.

Notes: The park is open from dawn to dusk. There are no rest room facilities, but there is a public telephone. Picnicking, camping, and swimming arc prohibited. Dogs are not allowed on the property.

3. Mount Algo

Type:	Dayhike
Difficulty:	Difficult for children
Distance:	3 miles, loop
Hiking time:	3.5 hours
High point/elevation gain:	1125 feet, 750 feet
Hikable:	May–November
Maps:	USGS Kent

Why did we decide to include Connecticut's toughest hiking trail in our guide? Because it was there. You and your older kids will feel exhilarated (as well as exhausted) after completing the state's longest, steepest climb. Every bit as challenging as it sounds, this trail is inappropriate for small children or anyone who is not in very good physical condition. Once part of the Appalachian Trail, it is now a trail maintained by the nearby Kent School. (Indians on the abutting reservation no longer allow hikers to walk on the portion of trail that crosses their land.)

 From the junction of US 7 and CT-341 in Kent, drive west on CT-341 over the Housatonic River. The first paved road on the left after the bridge is River Road. Park at the corner and walk

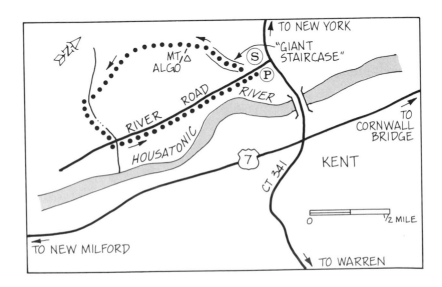

0.2 mile down River Road, where the red-blazed trail heads steeply into the woods on the right.

The trail (marked with red blazes painted over white ones) starts off at a 60-degree angle and climbs steadily upward for 30 feet then turns left, heading along a hillside over large boulders. In 100 yards, the trail ascends sharply again, twisting and turning, squeezing between slabs of rock. Count your steps on what has been dubbed the "Giant Staircase" so that kids will feel an increasing sense of accomplishment. Fallen boulders create small caves waiting to be explored by curious hikers.

Climbing at close to a 45-degree angle for most of this initial section, the path snakes past the boulder field, inching its way to

View over the Housatonic River Valley from the trail to Mount Algo

the summit of Mount Algo at 0.4 mile. At the top of the ridge, a blue-blazed trail heads left; you stay to the right on the red trail. Soon the path drops moderately into the valley between the two ridges. Just 0.3 mile from the summit, you will hear the sound of rushing water and notice that the trail has widened to become a tote road carved into the side of the ridge. Continue the moderately steep descent as the sound of the stream intensifies. Soon you will arrive at a series of cascades. Water tumbles through a narrow ravine to a brook that feeds the Housatonic River. Crossing this brook over a hodgepodge of logs and stones is tricky in spring or after a heavy rain. Kids will need a hand. Just after this crossing, in a stand of evergreens near the brook, you might catch your breath while the kids play games in the shallow water. The trail weaves beside the river (some white blazes are interspersed with the red) and emerges onto River Road. Turn left (north) and walk 1.2 miles to your car parked at the intersection of River Road and CT-341.

---

4. Northeast Audubon Center

Type: Dayhike
Difficulty: Easy for children
Distance: 1.5 miles, loop
Hiking time: 1 hour
High point/elevation gain: 1050 feet, 140 feet
Hikable: Year-round
Maps: USGS Ellsworth

Need a hiking suggestion for an overcast day? Try the Northeast Audubon Center in Sharon. The captivating views along the Bog Meadow and Fern trails are short range, so a few clouds won't detract from your enjoyment. And, on a dreary day, you may have the place to yourself. These paths take you past two ponds teeming with wildlife—primarily geese, ducks, and beavers (we saw a swan)—through some spacious meadows and dense woods known to house deer, foxes, coyotes, and bobcats. All the kids—from toddlers to teenagers—will have fun on this walk. One of five national nature centers owned by the National Audubon Society, this property is comprised of some 684 acres with 11

Boardwalk near Bog Meadow Pond

miles of hiking trails. The nature museum features live reptiles
and amphibians and an indoor honey-bee hive.

From the junction of US 7 and CT-4 in Cornwall Bridge,
drive west on CT-4 for 7 miles and watch for the Audubon Center
signs on the left leading to the parking area.

From the large wooden trail map at the far end of the parking
area, head southeast on the Lucy Harvey Trail to the Bog
Meadow and Fern trails. At the junction with the Bog Meadow
Road, turn right past the spillway of Ford Pond. An old ice house

35

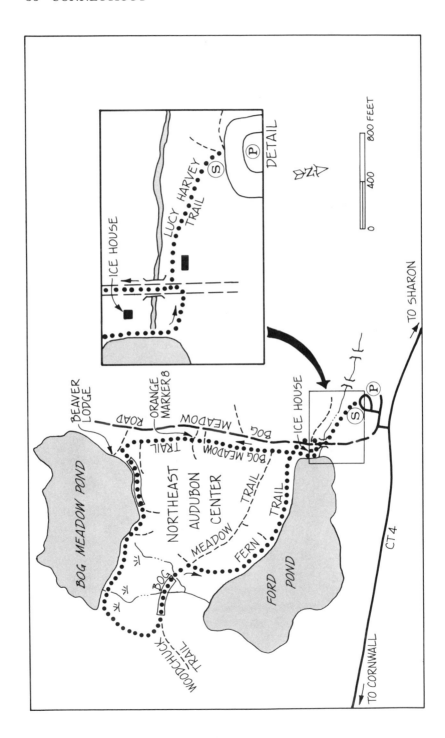

perched near the spillway dates from the days when this 30-acre pond was used for ice harvesting. In less than 100 yards, turn left at the sign indicating the way to Bog Meadow and Fern trails and then right onto Bog Meadow Trail. As you pass Ford Pond, the trail splits: The Fern Trail heads left, but you should follow the Bog Meadow Trail to the right. The path winds through a mixed hardwood and evergreen forest along a rocky path. In the fall, the kids can collect multicolored leaves along the trail.

Soon, the Bog Meadow Trail divides (it makes a loop); follow the right-hand path as it climbs gradually and then levels off. At orange marker 8, walk through an opening in a stone wall and cross a field on a mowed path. (Keep the kids on the path because the meadow is a popular nesting spot for birds.) Less than 0.3 mile from the split in the Bog Meadow Trail, you will reach Bog Meadow Pond. Turn left. (A right turn here will bring you to water's edge and a large abandoned beaver lodge.) The kids can keep an eye out for signs of beaver activity: dams and gnawed tree stumps. In the spring, look into the shallow water for the eggs of frogs and toads. Frogs lay their eggs in a large, jelly-coated mass while toads lay theirs in a long, thin ribbon.

Head quietly across a boardwalk and then follow the soggy path that squeezes between the pond's edge on the right and a bog on the left. You may see a river otter if you don't make too much noise. Pause and listen to the birds and bullfrogs. Smell the skunk cabbage plants that punctuate the lush vegetation by the pond. At the intersection with the Woodchuck Trail, turn left, remaining on the Bog Meadow Trail. Though occasional arrows guide your way, the worn trail is obvious and easy to follow. After crossing a swamp along another boardwalk, turn right at a four-way intersection to join the Fern Trail. As you head north along the Fern Trail, you'll soon glimpse Ford Pond through the trees. Kids may stumble along this rocky and rooted trail, especially if they are watching ducks floating on the pond. Fern Trail exits onto the beginning of Bog Meadow Trail. Turn right and walk along the top of the dam at the head of Ford Pond. Rest on the wrought iron bench and enjoy the pretty pond views (look for swans!) before returning to your car on the Lucy Harvey Trail.

Notes: The Audubon Society charges a moderate admission per person for nonmembers. Trails are open dawn to dusk. The buildings (including a museum and store) are open Monday through Saturday, 9:00 a.m. to 5:00 p.m., and Sunday, 1:00 p.m. to 5:00 p.m. They are closed on major holidays.

5. Dean Ravine and Barrack Mountain

Type: Dayhike or overnight
Difficulty: Difficult for children
Distance: 3.8 miles, round trip
Hiking time: 3.5 hours
High point/elevation gain: 1140 feet, 750 feet
Hikable: April–November
Maps: USGS South Canaan

In New England, they say that if today's weather doesn't suit you, just wait a few weeks—it's sure to change. On this hike, if a particular section of trail doesn't inspire you, just walk a few tenths of a mile—it'll change. Climb from a cool ravine through a heavily wooded section across a boulder field to a steep, exposed ridge. Even the temperature changes as you hike from the "air-conditioned" ravine to the exposed summit. This hike holds something for everyone, provided "everyone" is outfitted with proper hiking gear and has had some trail experience.

 From the junction of CT-112 and US 7 near Lime Rock, drive north on US 7 across the Housatonic River and in 0.2 mile turn right onto Lime Rock Station Road following signs to Music Mountain. In 0.9 mile, turn left onto Music Mountain Road still following signs to Music Mountain. In another 0.8 mile, at a junction with Cream Hill Road, park on the left. (No overnight parking.)

The trail leads northward from the back of the parking area, immediately joining the blue-blazed Mohawk Trail. Continue north then curl west, guided by a trail sign leading hikers down into the ravine that cradles a swiftly moving stream. Under a thick canopy of hemlocks, the brook spawns numerous whirlpools on its descent. What happens to sticks and leaves tossed into the hurrying brook? The trail plunges to the depths of the ravine, temporarily departing the riverbank to skirt a dropoff with scenic falls and a cascade. The footpath rejoins the brook at the bottom of the cascade. If the day is steamy and hot, pause here to drink in the gorge's cool, damp air. Wander along the stream for 0.5 mile until you come to a camping area (stoves only; no open fires). Here, the stream opens up into a series of wading pools.

In Dean Ravine

The trail now bends away from the stream and merges onto Music Mountain Road. Turn right (west) onto this paved road and in 0.15 mile, turn right again, reentering the woods (double blue blazes mark a telephone pole on the opposite side of the road).

TO SOUTH CANAAN

BARRACK MOUNTAIN

CREAM HILL ROAD

7

DEAN RAVINE

S

P

TO LIME ROCK & WEST CORNWALL

LIME ROCK STATION

MUSIC MT. RD.

ROAD

0   ½ MILE

Climb moderately on the wooded ridge heading north and east. After a short plateau, climb along a second rocky ridge. Beyond this second ridge, the path threads its way through a brief, boulder-strewn section, reminiscent of the trails that wind through the White Mountains of New Hampshire. The trail then veers left and descends for 0.2 mile. If you time your hike just right, the distant roar of cars racing at Lime Rock mingles with the subtler sounds of the forest. After traveling briefly on level ground, the trail begins a moderate ascent.

CAUTION Approaching the summit of Barrack Mountain, the trail traverses the top of a 30-foot rock cliff, turns right, and then left and scales a steep slope to the top of the ridge. Here, the expansive southwesterly vistas are the first unobstructed views along this route. Beyond this overlook, a ravine cuts into the mountain on the left and you'll pass by a rocky ledge that juts out to create a tunnel leading into the gorge. On the final climb to the peak, you must lean hard into the hill; scrambling on all fours may be the easiest way to scale the slope. Give younger kids a hand and older ones a word of encouragement. Nearly 2 miles from the start, from Barrack Mountain's bald face, the rolling hills of Connecticut stretch before you. Spread out the picnic lunch while the kids watch the races at Lime Rock through the binoculars. Can anyone see Paul Newman, Lime Rock's most famous driver? With caution and patience, climb down the mountain the way you came. It's a tough descent, so be sure to allow the kids the time they need to establish solid footing. When you reach the car, be sure to compliment everyone on a hike well done.

6. Pine Knob/Housatonic Meadows State Park

Type: Dayhike or overnight
Difficulty: Moderate for children
Distance: 2.9 miles, loop
Hiking time: 2.25 hours
High point/elevation gain: 1160 feet, 700 feet
Hikable: March–December
Maps: USGS Ellsworth

Was the Pine Cobble hike (hike 37) in Williamstown, Massachusetts, one of your favorites? Then you and your family are sure to enjoy the trip to Pine Knob, similar in many ways to its Massachusetts cousin. The ascent is nearly identical, as is the return trip, with one added attraction: a lovely, cascading trailside stream. Though the top of Pine Knob isn't quite as exposed as the rocky Pine Cobble crest, the views from these two summits of

An extra hand helps on the ascent to Pine Knob.

nearby valleys surrounded by layers of rolling hills are very much alike. Parents—especially those intending to backpack small children—must be aware of an unavoidable 10-foot drop that requires hikers to inch down a rock face using limited footholds. Although little hikers will be able to manage the ascent to Pine Knob, this compulsory maneuver on the way down may require more skill than they have, making this an inappropriate hike for them. Riverbank campsites are available at the nearby Housatonic Meadows Campground.

 From the junction of CT-4 and US 7 in Cornwall, take US 7 north for 1 mile to a parking area (for dayhikers only) on the left (notice a blue oval sign for the Pine Knob Loop Trail).

Locate the blue-blazed trail heading into the woods from the northeastern end of the parking area. Walk along Hatch Brook, sweeping past an old cellar hole and curving right to cross the brook on well-positioned rocks. In the spring, only the quick and surefooted hiker will keep his or her feet dry here. The trail approaches and passes through a break in a wandering stone wall at a wooden trail map. Here, at a trail junction, you turn right on the blue trail as the red path heads left. At 0.2 mile, the Pine Knob Loop Trail officially begins: at this intersection, continue straight, heading north on blue blazes. The trail parallels US 7,

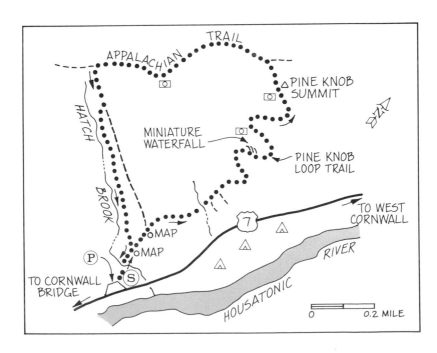

traveling on relatively flat ground through a pine and hemlock forest. After fording a stream, pass side trails leading to US 7 and the Housatonic Meadows Campground. Four-tenths of a mile from the start of the loop, the trail swings left at double blazing and begins its assault on Pine Knob. Two-tenths of a mile into the moderately steep ascent, a miniature waterfall gushes over a rock mass. Who will be the first young hiker to reach this pleasant resting spot?

As you approach the summit, the smooth, gravel path becomes increasingly rockier and more root-choked due to erosion on this upper slope. At 1 mile, the trail opens up to the first of two lookouts with fine southeasterly views of adjoining hills. The path continues, winding through thickets of mountain laurel and traversing a boulder field that necessitates some scrambling. Soon, you will arrive at a second vista, 1.1 miles from the start, with southeasterly panoramas including Mohawk Mountain. (If you wish to avoid the precarious dropoff mentioned in the opening paragraph, turn around here and retrace your steps to your car.) Beyond this second overlook, climb 0.1 mile to the wooded summit with limited northerly views. Here, a sheer drop down a 10-foot-high rock face will challenge even the most skilled hiker. Carefully inch your way down this rock wall and rejoin the path along flatter terrain.

Shortly, at a junction, turn left, continuing to follow the blue-blazed Pine Knob Loop Trail that has been joined by the renowned Appalachian Trail, blazed in white. If the kids are beginning to complain, remind them that many of the hikers who marched along this same path did so en route from Georgia to Maine, walking every mile of the Appalachian Trail's 2050 miles, the longest continuously marked trail in the world. After 0.4 mile of easy walking, you'll arrive at another overlook where views of the Housatonic Valley stretch before you. Descend southwest to a branch in the trail at 2 miles; the Appalachian Trail departs on the right while you curl left along the blue-blazed loop trail approaching Hatch Brook, a tributary of the Housatonic River. In approximately 0.1 mile, at triple red blazes, turn right to follow along the riverbank on the red-blazed trail as the blue-blazed trail bears left away from the brook. The trail descends moderately through this hemlock ravine, following closely along the edge of the cascading brook. Kids will have fun racing with stick and leaf boats. The red trail leaves you at the stone wall and trail map. Turn right through the opening in the wall to return to your car.

The stone tower on the way to Mohawk Mountain's summit offers a place to relax and daydream.

7. Mohawk Mountain

Type:	Dayhike or overnight
Difficulty:	Moderate for children
Distance:	5.5 miles, loop
Hiking time:	4 hours
High point/elevation gain:	1683 feet, 700 feet
Hikable:	April–November
Maps:	USGS Cornwall

You know this park as a terrific place for winter sports, but did you realize that Mohawk's trail system is also superb? The extensive views of the western highlands from Mohawk's 1683-foot

summit not only have been admired by hikers but also put to
practical use since Colonial days. Centuries ago, Tunxis and
Paugussett Indians sent smoke signals from the mountaintop to
warn fellow tribesmen of any aggressive moves made by the enemy Mohawks (thus, the name of the mountain). In recent years,
rangers have scanned the hillsides from the summit lookout
tower for forest fires. The facilities here are extensive, ranging
from frequent trailside wells and springs to outhouses, lookout
towers, and picnic and camping sites. So, if you've only thought to
visit Mohawk Mountain after the first snowfall, think again!

From the junction of CT-63 and CT-4 in Goshen (at a rotary),
travel west on CT-4 for 4 miles to the entrance to Mohawk State
Forest on the left.

Begin your hike at the information bulletin board just inside
the gate. Travel east on a dirt park road for approximately 100
yards to a light blue double blaze on the right that directs you
into the woods. (This is the Mohawk Trail joining you from the
north; be sure to head south along the path.) The path swerves to
the left of a lean-to and dips down into a damp area. In approximately 0.1 mile, the path abruptly swerves right to skirt a rock
outcrop. Notice the fissure to the left of this massive stone face—a
cave for the kids to explore? The trail ascends momentarily then
drops. At 0.8 mile, the footpath intersects a cross-country ski
trail. Here is where you'll rejoin the initial section of trail after
completing the loop. For now, continue straight, following the
blue blazes. Did you bring along a book of animal tracks? The
kids can look for indications of deer, bobcats, and fox.

Soon, you skirt the right-hand side of a second camping area,
with a lean-to, campfire sites, and picnic tables. When the trail
emerges onto Toumey Road at 1.3 miles, turn left (south) and, 0.1
mile later, turn right into the woods at double blue blazes. The
path leads through a red pine plantation and travels past the top
of the chairlifts for the ski area. Near the second lift, at 1.5 miles,
is a stone observation platform. From the platform you can see
across the expansive ski area to the distant mountains of Connecticut, New York, and Massachusetts.

Back at the second ski lift outlet, follow a jeep road as it
branches off from the blue trail to the left (south) at the second
chairlift outlet. A short descent leads to an intersection with the
Mattatuck Trail, also blue blazed. Head straight (southeast)
along the Mattatuck Trail, which shortly joins the Mattatuck
Road (the road to the summit). The trail follows the road southerly for a few yards then proceeds back into the woods, right, at

double blue blazes (this section of the trail may be rerouted during logging operations). In this area, you'll notice an extensive logging operation; diseased red pines are being removed to make room for young deciduous trees. After skirting a logged area, travel briefly through the woods and pass to the east of a massive stone tower. The path curls left away from the tower and crosses another logged area where the top of Mohawk Mountain is visible to the southeast. Plunging once more under the canopy of the forest, the trail snakes through a swampy area, crosses a stone wall and then a stream. Have thirsty kids keep an eye out for the spring. After cutting across another section of the wall, 2.2 miles from the start, you'll arrive at a pipe spewing icy spring water. The trail climbs to a gravel road, crosses the road and begins a moderate ascent with well-placed log and stone steps past an exposed ledge. Walk along rolling terrain with emerging views that promise even more dramatic vistas from the summit. Cross a grassy road and make your way along more exposed ledges. Turn right onto a gravel road, following the blue blazes to the summit and its lookout tower. Here, at 2.85 miles, enjoy the dramatic views and a picnic. Views to the north and west include the Taconic, Catskill, and Berkshire ranges. It won't be hard for kids to imagine the Tunxis Indians scanning the countryside for signs of the dreaded Mohawks.

To return, walk east down the paved Mattatuck Road and in 100 yards, at a hairpin turn, leave the road and continue straight into the woods on a rutted trail marked with yellow triangular blazes. At the gravel Wadhams Road at 3 miles, turn left. Follow this road for a total of 1 mile, passing access to a camping area on the left and maintenance buildings on the right before meeting the paved Mohawk Mountain Road. Turn right here. In 0.1 mile (just beyond another access for the maintenance buildings), a sign for a cross-country ski trail indicates a left-hand turn onto a grassy road. Follow this wide path, continuing straight across an intersection 0.1 mile later. Climb a short, steep hill to a split in the trail; follow the trail right, on a gradual incline, while the left-hand path drops to a swamp. Watch for the occasional plastic markers with a skiing figure. Climb to the height of a hill, sidestep Mohawk Mountain Road, and drop to a T intersection with another cross-country ski trail; turn left. At the 4.7-mile mark, turn right at the intersection with the Mohawk Trail. Follow this blue-blazed trail to your car, 0.8 mile away.

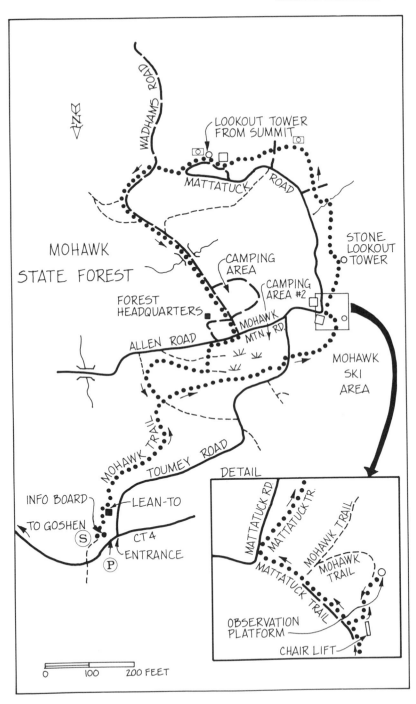

8. William Buell Natural Area

Type: Dayhike
Difficulty: Easy for children
Distance: 2 miles, round trip
Hiking time: 1.5 hours
High point/elevation gain: 1150 feet, 200 feet
Hikable: March–November
Maps: USGS West Torrington

Even folks who are Litchfield born and bred aren't aware that this property exists, making a hike along the scenic gorge feel like a true journey through the wilderness. Whose child isn't

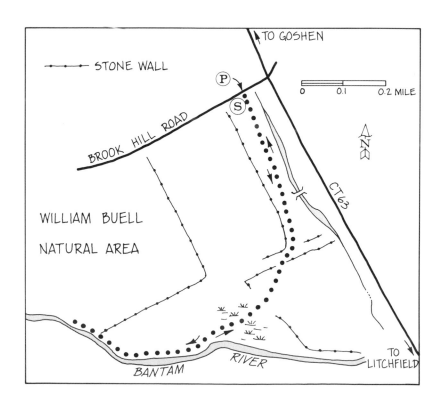

mesmerized by water crashing down cascade after cascade in a never-ending race with no one? Though the trail is overgrown in places, it is clearly blazed and follows along the river bank for much of its length. This is a great spur-of-the-moment trip for any family in the area with a free afternoon. Put the kids in sneakers and long pants and go!

From Litchfield center, drive north on CT-63 for 3.4 miles to the Goshen/Litchfield town line and Brook Hill Road on the left. (Notice the yellow and green Nature Conservancy signs posted on trees along CT-63 just before Brook Hill Road.) Turn left (west) and drive just 300 feet down Brook Hill Road and park on the side of the road.

The white-blazed trail runs south from the road between two birch trees, at the end of the cable-and-post fence. The path, while not well traveled, is still easy to follow. For 0.35 mile, it runs parallel to CT-63 with a stone wall bordering the west side. As another wall joins from the east, turn right. Shortly, turn left

Pausing to admire the cascades along the Bantam River

through an opening in this second stone wall. As you head away from the highway, the noise of cars is gradually drowned out by the sounds of the roaring Bantam River. The overgrown path plunges into several swampy areas brimming with skunk cabbage, a common plant that thrives in wetland areas. Its characteristic large green leaves emit a smell similar to a skunk's when broken off. Have the kids break off a leaf and sniff to discover how this malodorous plant got its name. The trail reaches the river at the 0.6-mile mark and follows along its bank for 0.4 mile. Kids can toss small sticks or leaves into the water and watch as their boats are rushed downstream, dodging some rocks and tumbling over others. Triple blazes mark the end of the trail, at which point you reverse direction and return to your car by the same trail.

9. The White Memorial Foundation

Type:	Dayhike or overnight (with advance reservations)
Difficulty:	Easy for children
Distance:	2.2 miles, loop
Hiking time:	2 hours
High point/elevation gain:	980 feet, 140 feet
Hikable:	Year-round
Maps:	USGS Litchfield

Even with 4000 acres and 35 miles of trails and woodland roads, the nature museum may be the feature that appeals most to children visiting "White's Woods." The exhibits are fascinating (including live animals and electric board games), and the nature library on the second floor, one of the best in the state, contains a special section for children. Other features that attract families to the property are its two campgrounds, the most popular being Point Folly, a peninsula that juts into Bantam Lake and offers campsites at water's edge.

From the junction of US 202 and CT-63 in Litchfield center, drive south on US 202 for about 2 miles to Bissell Road on the left. Turn here and then make an immediate right onto a gravel road

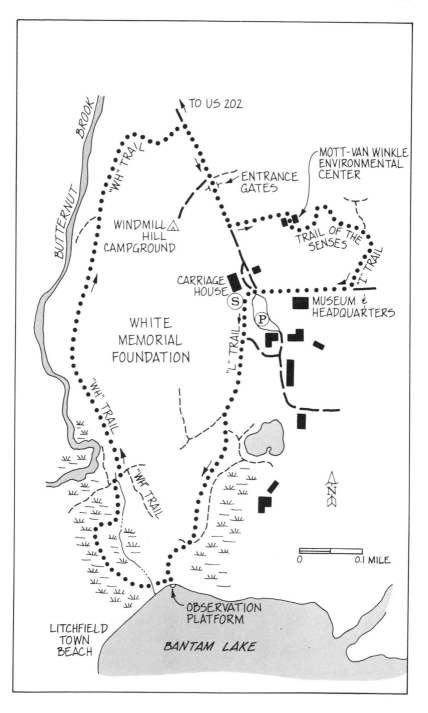

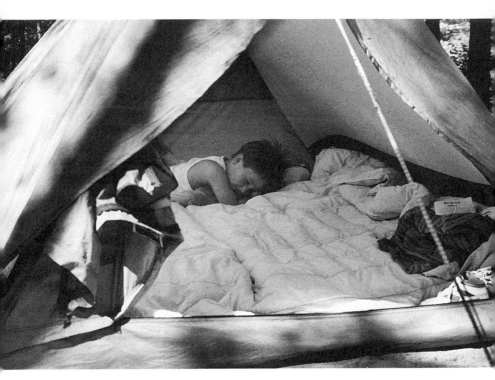

ZZZZZZZZ

that leads in 0.5 mile to the White Memorial Foundation head-quarters and parking area.

Begin on the L Trail near the carriage house. Follow the yellow rectangular blazes along the edge of a field and enter the woods through a gate on a wide, grassy path. Let the kids run ahead. At two junctions with woods roads, bear left, and ignore foot trails that branch off to the left. The easy-to-follow trail descends very gradually, heading south, and in 0.5 mile reaches Bantam Lake. Turn right to reach the observation platform. Give each of the kids a turn looking through the binoculars at the ducks and other water birds that frequent the area. Continue west along the L Trail, now a footpath, through wetlands. Watch for swamp sparrows, yellow warblers, and red-winged blackbirds. Tell the kids to keep an eye out for signs of muskrats and beavers. In the summertime, you may be able to hear the faraway sounds of children playing at the Litchfield Town Beach.

Three-tenths of a mile from the lake, the trail intersects a woods road. Turn right and quickly left onto a green-blazed trail, the WH Trail, and follow this grassy, woods road in a northerly direction for 0.7 mile until you reach the entrance road. Turn right onto the road and walk through the entrance gates. Behind the buildings of the Mott-Van Winkle Environmental Center (down a side road to the left), locate the trail head for the Trail of the Senses, which shortly merges with the I (Interpretive Nature) Trail. This level, easy trail has 17 numbered stations corresponding to descriptions in a brochure available (for a small price) in the main building. Turn right onto the I Trail and in 0.3 mile you will return to the museum and the parking lot.

10. Mount Tom Tower

Type: Dayhike
Difficulty: Moderate for children
Distance: 1 mile, loop
Hiking time: 1.5 hours
High point/elevation gain: 1291 feet, 400 feet
Hikable: April–November
Maps: USGS New Preston

This short hike is still a challenging one for small hikers because you will gain 400 feet within 0.5 mile. The summit, at 1291 feet, stands more than 100 feet higher than the Massachusetts mountain that shares its name. The climb through dense forest culminates in a fabulous view from atop the stone tower. After the hike, the whole family can take a dive into the pristine water of Mount Tom Pond and then finish the day with a beachside picnic. Toilets, changing houses, and drinking water are available near the beach. (If you hike mid-winter, bring your ice skates and explore the pond Dorothy Hamill-style at the end of your walk.)

From the junction of US 202 and CT-63 in Litchfield center, drive 6.3 miles south on US 202. Pass Mount Tom Pond on the the left, with Mount Tom rising over the water. Turn left at the sign for Mount Tom and in 100 yards a "Mount Tom State Park Entrance" sign indicates another left-hand turn. Drive past a booth (in the summer, you will have to pay a small fee per car during the week, and a bit more on weekends). In 0.2 mile, park near a large, wooden trail map sign.

At the trail plaque, begin your ascent on a trail marked with yellow blazes. Within 0.1 mile, you will pass an old foundation and stone fireplace on the left. This is all that is left of Camp Sepunkum, a Boy Scout camp dating from the early 1900s. The fireplace once heated the scouts' assembly hall. Avoiding unblazed sidetrails, continue to follow the rocky and rugged, well-worn path to the summit. In 0.2 mile, a second yellow-blazed trail joins the first. Bear left here and also at the second intersection with the yellow trail, 0.1 mile later. The trail curls roughly to the mountaintop, cutting through swampy areas and crossing streams by way of stepping stones. Take turns leading the way, with the group following directly in the leader's footsteps (it's more fun that way).

In about 0.4 mile, you will reach the summit and the stone tower. The view from the ground here is limited but side paths lead to overlooks and the view from the top of the tower, at 1325 feet, is magnificent. (Children will need help climbing the stairs

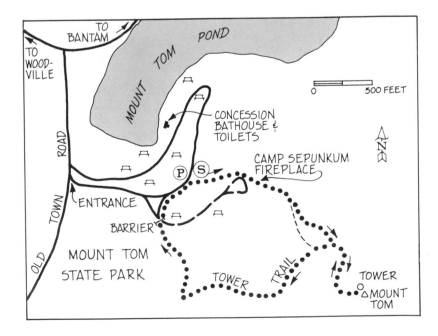

View of Connecticut's rolling hills from the Mount Tom Tower

because there are no railings; warn taller kids to watch their heads on the final set of steps.) When this cement and bluestone tower was being built in 1921, horses had to pull wagons full of sand, water, stones, and cement up the side of the mountain. Look to the northwest to see Bear Mountain (Connecticut's highest peak) and the Mount Riga Range and nearby Mount Everett in Massachusetts. On the descent along the Tower Trail, bear left within the first 0.2 mile at two junctions with yellow-blazed paths and arrive at the base of the mountain near a barrier. Head down a dirt road through a picnic area and turn right onto a paved road; walk 100 yards to the trail head or head straight for the lake.

Exploring the legendary Leatherman Cave

11. Leatherman Cave

Type: Dayhike
Difficulty: Moderate for children
Distance: 2 miles, round trip
Hiking time: 1.5 hours
High point/elevation gain: 860 feet, 450 feet
Hikable: April–November
Maps: USGS Thomaston

Little is known about the peculiar man for whom this cave is named. He was said to be Jules Bourglay, who left his home in Lyons, France, when his poor financial judgment ruined the family leather business and his future wife left him. Dressed completely in leather clothing (which was estimated to weigh 60 pounds) and sleeping only in caves, he roamed Connecticut for nearly 30 years in the late 1800s. He refused to sleep in barns or homes but did accept food handouts, expressing his thanks with grunts. His body was eventually found in a cave near Ossining, New York. The trip along the Mattatuck Trail to Leatherman Cave, one of this wanderer's favorite resting places, offers breathtaking views of the nearby rolling hills. Be warned, however, that these panoramas are from atop precipitous cliffs at trail's edge. Kids who are not "trail-wise" should postpone this hike until they have more experience.

From the intersection of CT-109 and US 6 in Thomaston, drive southwest on US 6. In 0.5 mile, you will pass Black Rock State Park and at 0.9 mile, look on the right-hand side of the road for a blue oval marker indicating a junction with the Mattatuck Trail. Park off the road near the sign.

Cross the road to begin the hike, heading southeast. The blue-blazed Mattatuck Trail leads through a pine grove and ascends on a narrow, rocky path. Often traversing large expanses of rock that sparkle with mica chips, the path curls upward, tucked into the forest between boulders and mountain laurel. Within the first 0.4 mile, you will travel along a precipitous ledge with stunning views of the nearby hills. These panoramas will convince you that a series of rolling hills (especially in autumn) can look just as awesome to a hiker as a giant ice-capped mountain. To the left of the trail is a sheer drop of at least 65 feet, so hold the hand

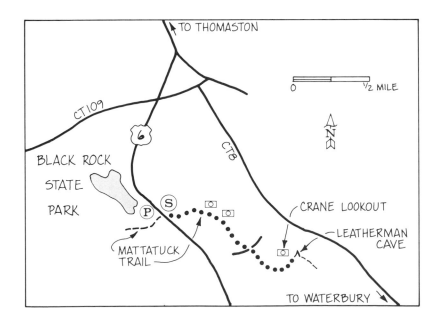

of any child who isn't surefooted. Look southeasterly across the canyon at the barren hill (the result of a forest fire several years ago); this is your destination. Continue to follow the rutted, blue-blazed trail as it winds downhill through the woods. (Side trails enter and exit, so watch for the blue blazes.) Turn left onto a jeep trail at the 0.6-mile mark; in about 100 yards, turn right onto a trail that begins a moderate climb. Nearly 1 mile into the hike, you will reach Crane Lookout with more lovely views. Leatherman Cave is at the southern base of this overlook. This rock labyrinth with its dark tunnels and mysterious passageways will keep the kids intrigued long enough to allow the adults to set out a picnic lunch on the grassy hill nearby. When you're ready, retrace your steps through the woods and along the ridge back to your car.

12. Mad River and Buttermilk Falls

Type:	Dayhike
Difficulty:	Moderate for children
Distance:	3.3 miles, one way
Hiking time:	2.5 hours, one way
High point/elevation gain:	900 feet, 175 feet
Hikable:	April–November
Maps:	USGS Southington and Bristol

Buttermilk Falls is a popular attraction with townspeople as well as visitors to the area. But although you may meet up with some other families at this well-known local landmark, you will probably have the hike along Mad River to yourself. The falls are accessible by car, just off of Lane Hill Road. In fact, we recommend that you leave a second car here because it would be quite tiring for the younger members of the family to make the return trip (and tiring for parents to listen to their tired children).

 First car: From the junction of CT-69 and CT-322 in Wolcott, travel north on CT-69. In approximately 0.25 mile, turn left onto Mad River Road following signs for Wolcott-Peterson Park. In 0.25 mile, you will see tennis courts on the right and a sign for

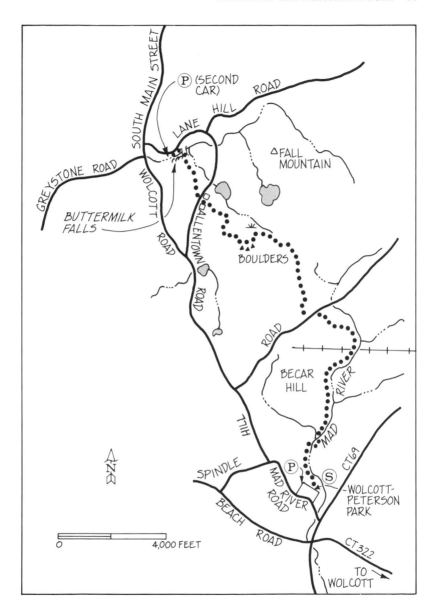

Wolcott-Peterson Park. The blue-blazed Mattatuck Trail heads
right down the entrance road to the park. Leave your car near the
basketball courts.

Second car: Take a right out of the parking area for Wolcott-
Peterson Park. Travel 0.4 mile down Mad River Road and turn

Picnic lunch beside Buttermilk Falls

right onto Spindle Hill Road. At the next intersection (1 mile), go straight on what is now Allentown Road. At 2 miles, continue straight again as the road becomes Wolcott Road. At 2.8 miles, turn right onto South Main Street. Take a right-hand turn onto Lane Hill Road at 2.9 miles and drive 500 feet. Park at a sign for Buttermilk Falls on the right side of the road.

Back at the first parking area, pick up the blue trail on the left-hand (northern) side of the park's basketball courts. (Note that double blazes are used along this trail even for gentle turns.) For the first 1.1 miles, follow along the bank of Mad River, which drops gradually in a series of small cascades. The kids can race twig boats down the swiftly moving river. At about the 0.4-mile mark, they will need help crossing from the riverbank to a peninsula and back. The trail soon emerges onto an open field, ducks under power lines, and sweeps left away from the river onto a jeep road. Shortly, turn left onto a foot path (still following the blue-blazed Mattatuck Trail) and climb a hill, diving back into the woods. The trail winds through the forest for 0.2 mile then drops down a steep hill under a canopy of rhododendrons.

At 1.7 miles, the path outlets onto Spindle Hill Road. Turn left and in 200 feet, rejoin the blue-blazed trail as it heads back into the woods from the right-hand side of the road. Follow the meandering path through the woods to a swampy area, 2.4 miles from the start. With the wetlands on the right and unusual rock formations bordering the trail's left side, urge the kids to run ahead until they arrive at more dramatic trailside boulders. Continue to a logged area, skirting the left-hand side. Soon, the path breaks into a residential area, darting between two homes to reach Allentown Road. Head diagonally right across the road and reenter the woods, winding through a mixed hardwood forest for 0.2 mile until a steep descent leads to a river crossing on a wooden bridge. Turn left and travel along the rocky bank of the river rushing toward Buttermilk Falls. The boulders lining the falls offer front-row seats to those who want to admire nature at her best. From the falls, follow the blue blazes for a short distance to the road and your second car.

13. Burr Pond State Park

Type: Dayhike
Difficulty: Easy for children
Distance: 3 miles, loop
Hiking time: 2 hours
High point/elevation gain: 1080 feet, 170 feet
Hikable: Year-round
Maps: USGS Torrington

Nestled in the hills of northwestern Connecticut, Burr Pond State Park is the site of Borden's first condensed milk factory, built in 1854. The well-worn Wolcott Trail encircles the 88-acre Burr Pond, passing by glacial boulders once used as Indian caves and leading through a public park with a sandy beach. Wear your bathing suit under your shorts and t-shirt so that you will be ready for a swim here, close to the end of the hike. This is a can't-get-lost trip—just keep the shoreline in sight on your left and you'll eventually return to your starting point. Even in wintertime, this is a pretty hike: The surroundings never seem barren and bleak with the dense hemlock forests and colonies of mountain laurel ensuring year-round color. Burr Pond State Park offers 40 campsites at its Taylor Brook Campground.

From CT-8 in Torrington, take Exit 46 to Pinewoods Road,. Burrville. Travel west 0.3 mile to an intersection and turn left onto Winsted Road, following a sign to Burr Pond. In 0.9 mile, turn right at a blinking light onto Burr Mountain Road. In 0.5 mile, pass the entrance to Burr Pond State Park and drive 0.2 mile further to a boat launch parking lot on the left.

The hike begins on the west side of the parking lot, 50 yards from water's edge, on a trail blazed with black and gray paint. Head in a northwesterly direction with the pond on your left. Within the first 0.1 mile, the trail curls to the left (southwest) and crosses a small stream by way of a footbridge. The narrow gravel trail hugs the shoreline initially, passing through a hemlock grove and thick stands of mountain laurel. If you are hiking during the colder months, the kids may be surprised that the laurel bushes have remained green. Have them touch the leaves. The waxy coating shields the leaves from the effects of freezing temperatures. And the leaves are poisonous to many animals, so even during the winter when food is scarce, these bushes do not tempt deer and other wildlife.

Cross another stream at the 0.3-mile mark and then weave through a wetlands area on a plank walk. Alert the kids that the worn boards can be slippery. More footbridges cross slow-moving streams within the next 0.2 mile. At these frequent stream crossings, the children may want to stop for a few minutes to examine a frog or coax a turtle out of its shell. It's a three-mile walk around the pond, so frequent stops now will help conserve energy. As the path travels through a clearing cut for power lines, hikers are treated to a panoramic view of the pond. At the far end of the clearing, another stream meanders past.

As the path travels along the southwestern end of the pond, the trail climbs a small hill (the hike's only notable elevation gain). At light blue double blazes 1 mile from the start, turn left to remain on the Wolcott Trail. (The blue-blazed John Muir Trail heads right, eventually leading to Sunnybrook Park.) The path drops along rugged terrain, soon leveling out and passing within 100 feet of Big Rock Cave Lookout at 1.1 miles. Take a vote: Do your kids think this dramatic boulder resembles a fish head or candle flame? After traveling under the power lines once more, an unmarked side trail leads to Burr Point. This trail weaves through thickets of mountain laurel (spectacular in June when the plants blossom) and over exposed granite. Listen and look for signs of woodpeckers. The tip of the peninsula, at 1.4 miles, is an

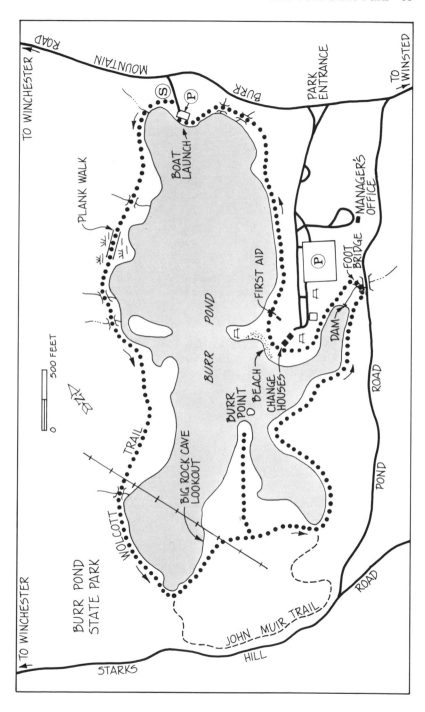

Canoeists on Burr Pond

ideal spot for a picnic lunch. Although the nearby public beach offers picnic tables and manicured lawns, here your family will enjoy a peaceful and solitary meal.

Leave the point and return to the main trail, turning left (southeast). At a second set of light blue double blazes (another junction with the John Muir Trail), turn left to head northeast, then north. The trail winds along the water's edge on a rock-laden bank and arrives at a dam with water spilling over the top at 2.2 miles. As the trail sweeps past the dam, a solid footbridge carries you across the river that feeds the pond. Bending left (west), the path follows the shoreline and cuts through the beach and picnic area, just 0.6 mile from your car. Here, the comforts of civilization await you: a telepone, rest rooms, a concession stand, and a first-aid station. Drinking water is available at several spots near the beach. Peel off that hiking gear and dive in! (Lifeguards are on duty from 10:00 a.m. to 6:00 p.m.) Beyond this busy spot, the trail leads through the woods past picnic sites that are not used as much, following along the water back to the boat launch area and your car. (You may wish to begin and end the hike from the parking area near the public beach. You will pay a parking fee in season and pets and alcoholic beverages are not allowed at the beach.)

14. Jessie Gerard Trail

Type: Dayhike
Difficulty: Moderate for children
Distance: 3.5 miles, round trip
Hiking time: 3 hours
High point/elevation gain: 1120 feet, 400 feet
Hikable: April–October
Maps: USGS New Hartford

The Jessie Gerard Trail is one of many interesting paths that wander through the 3000-acre Peoples State Forest. Each trail is named for an individual who played a significant role in acquiring or developing the land for the park. The Jessie Gerard Trail

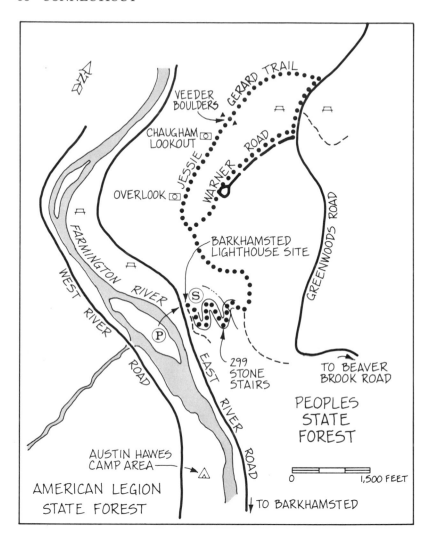

begins at the site of an old Indian settlement known as Barkhamsted Lighthouse near East River Road and climbs to an overlook by way of 299 stone steps. Challenging climbs, pleasant
forest surroundings, and magnificent views from two overlooks
make this a great hike for families in good condition with some
previous experience. Although no camping is allowed at Peoples
State Forest, the neighboring American Legion State Forest (just
across the Farmington River) does have camping facilities.

From US 44 in Barkhamsted, turn northeast onto CT-181/
CT-318, following signs to Peoples State Forest. In 0.7 mile, after

Hikers along the Jessie Gerard Trail

crossing the Farmington River, turn left (north) on East River Road. Travel 2.3 miles to a parking turnout on the left next to the river.

The trail begins on the opposite side of the road at two wooden posts bearing TRAIL signs. Fifty feet along, the yellow-blazed trail splits; you should bear left. The path climbs moderately, then more steeply for the first 0.3 mile as it travels up a wet ravine lined with the so-called 299 Stone Stairs. (The kids can try to keep count.) Above you, to the right, are huge rock walls that dazzle winter hikers with the natural ice sculptures that form as cascading water freezes in turquoise-colored masses. At the stream crossing, you are close to the crest of this rugged section. Soon, the yellow-blazed trail intersects a trail marked with blue blazes. Turn left on this path, now dotted with both yellow and blue blazes. After a modest 0.4-mile climb, the blue-blazed trail exits right. (You will later return by this trail.) Continue straight on the yellow blazes, still encountering some steep, rocky ascents.

Just over a mile from the start, you will reach a small clearing and an overlook with dizzying views of the adjacent ridges. Kids can enjoy the view from a distance while more sure-footed adults can venture closer to the edge of the cliff. The trail reenters the woods and travels atop the ridge, passing through stands of majestic evergreens over level ground. With little underbrush and a thick carpet of pine needles, children may be inclined to wander off the path in search of pine cones or other forest collectibles. Soon a second overlook, Chaugham Lookout, is reached at 1.4 miles with similar wide panoramas. As the trail crawls back into the forest, let the kids run ahead with instructions to wait for you when the trail passes between two car-sized twin boulders (called the "Veeder Boulders") in another 0.1 mile.

At the 1.9-mile mark, the yellow-blazed trail joins paved Greenwoods Road. Turn right and in 0.1 mile you will see a picnic area with reliable water. Stop here so the kids can take a breather and have a snack. Another 0.1 mile beyond the picnic area, you will pass by the yellow-blazed trail that turns left into the woods; continue walking straight on the paved road. As you approach the top of a short hill, turn right onto gravel Warner Road. Follow this lane for 0.5 mile to its end at a turnaround. A blue-blazed trail exits right from the beginning of the turnaround and in 0.2 mile rejoins the yellow trail. Turn left and hike the 0.5 mile back to your car.

15. Peak Mountain and Old Newgate Prison

Type: Dayhike
Difficulty: Moderate for children
Distance: 4 miles, loop
Hiking time: 3 hours
High point/elevation gain: 672 feet, 350 feet
Hikable: Late May–October
Maps: USGS Windsor Locks

A double feature is playing today in East Granby. First, a hike up to the overlook at Peak Mountain will provide lovely views of the rolling Connecticut countryside. Then, for your added enjoyment, a trek through the ruins of Old Newgate Prison will give kids a glimpse of what life was like as an eighteenth-century prisoner. The prison began as a copper mine in 1705. Nearly seventy years later, the Colony of Connecticut began to use the underground tunnels and hollows as dungeons for up to forty prisoners at a time. Many prisoners of war (such as British soldiers during the American Revolution) as well as common thieves and debtors were forced to toil in the mines of Newgate. Although the prison was abandoned in 1824 and many of the walls have crumbled, kids will still be able to imagine vividly the barbaric conditions these prisoners endured two centuries ago.

Take Exit 40 off of I-91 in Windsor Locks (the sign says "Old Newgate Prison—Seasonal"). Travel west 6.2 miles on CT-20, past the entrance to Bradley International Airport. Turn right (north) at a traffic light onto Newgate Road and immediately pull off the road onto the right-hand side.

The blue-blazed Metacomet Trail heads into the woods on the right, paralleling CT-20, and climbs steeply for 100 yards to a trail intersection. Turn left, continuing to watch for the blue blazes that will guide your way for the next 1.5 miles. The well-worn path weaves through a mixed hardwood forest on a gradual ascent. After climbing for about 1 mile, you will notice utility lines scaling the left-hand side of the hill. Here, the trail rises abruptly, requiring hikers to scramble for about 30 feet to reach

an outcropping with fine views to the west. You'll notice that the
utility lines that accompanied you on your hike up the mountain
service the signal lights on top of the ridge for airplanes flying in
and out of Bradley Airport. Is your son or daughter an airplane
buff? If so, he or she will delight in the distant drone of airplane
traffic overhead and identify the various aircraft for the rest of
you. Beyond the overlook, the trail reenters the woods on rolling
terrain and ascends abruptly to a second overlook.

After returning to the woods, the trail sweeps left on a short,
gradual descent and brings you to a small clearing at the edge of
the ridge, again providing views. Stop here, about 1.5 miles from
the start of the hike, and return to your car. From your car, you
may walk (1.1 mile) or drive to historic Old Newgate prison down
Old Newgate Road.

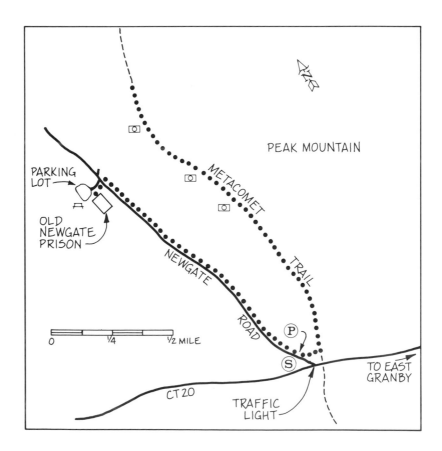

After your tour of the infamous dungeons, escape to the picnic tables perched on a hillside just outside the prison walls. Here, you can have lunch or just relax and enjoy the fine local views. Return to Newgate Road, turn right, and walk 1.1 miles to your car.

Notes: The prison is open to the public from mid-May or early June (it varies year to year) through the end of October. It is closed Mondays and Tuesdays, except on major holidays. Hours are 10:00 a.m. to 4:30 p.m. There is a moderate admission charge per person, though children under 6 are admitted free.

Inside the walls of Old Newgate Prison

16. Castle Crag and West Peak

Type: Dayhike
Difficulty: Difficult for children
Distance: 6 miles, round trip
Hiking time: 4.5 hours
High point/elevation gain: 1024 feet, 850 feet
Hikable: April–October
Maps: USGS Meriden

From atop the tower at Castle Crag, you will be able to see the Sleeping Giant hills to the south, the Metacomet ridges to the north, and, far away, Mount Tom in Massachusetts and the distant hills of the Holyoke range. Pick a clear day to hike this section of the Metacomet Trail to take full advantage of the views. It's fairly tough—long, with some steep climbs—so be prepared to carry small children who may tire out. But the stone lookout tower at Castle Crag is a perfect turnaround point for those who choose not to follow the path all the way to West Peak. As you drive along I-691, have the kids look for the "castle" perched on the side of the hill.

    From I-691 in Meriden, take Exit 4 (West Main Street). Turn east onto West Main Street and travel 0.7 mile to the entrance to Hubbard Park. Turn left into the park and follow the park road as it winds through the recreation area. At the first intersection, turn right and at the second, left, approaching the highway bridge. Travel under the bridge and through the gates onto Park Drive. At the far end of Merimere Reservoir, 1.7 miles from West Main Street, park on the right-hand side of the road at a barricaded intersection.

From the parking area, walk across the dam on Park Drive at the head of the reservoir. Here, at the reservoir's northern tip, the blue-blazed Metacomet Trail heads left off of the paved road into a gully, then climbs an embankment and dives into the woods. The trail ascends gradually then moderately over the 1.5-mile trek to Castle Crag. Initially, the trail leads through stands of evergreens along an often dormant stream that feeds the reservoir. In 0.3 mile, the trail curls left and follows above the reservoir.

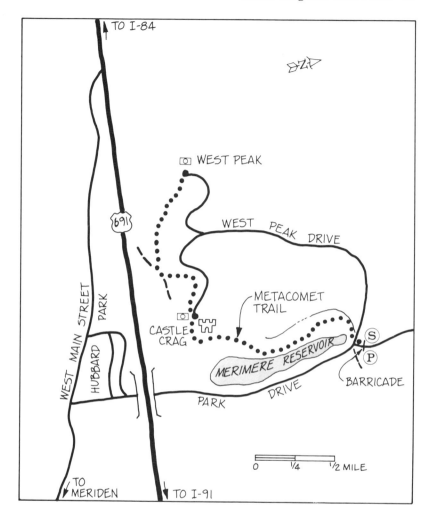

About halfway down the reservoir, the trail turns to the right, plunging deeper into the woods, and begins a series of stiffer ascents. To the right of the path, a thin stream flows through a shallow ravine. After about 0.5 mile of climbing, the trail again turns to the left, approaching the high ridge leading to Castle Crag. Soon, the trail flirts with the edge and provides fine views to the east over the adjacent ridge and to the south past the city of Meriden. Parents should take the hands of young hikers here.

As the trail begins to level out, traveling across rock out-

Tower at Castle Crag

crops, the views and the character of the ledges become more spectacular. Who will be the first to see the castle tower? As the tower comes into view, a rock peninsula juts out from the cliffs, reaching for the panoramas. It offers a picnic spot for those who don't suffer from vertigo. Soon, the Metacomet Trail emerges onto the eastern side of a parking lot. From here, walk to the stone tower set at the edge of a sheer cliff (at 976 feet above sea level) with breathtaking views east and south. You may have to vie for space in the tower with a few other folks who drove up West Peak Drive. Head back to your car the way you came for a total hike of 3 miles or continue another 1.5 miles to West Peak for a 6-mile round-trip total.

Back in the parking lot, facing the tower, search for the trail on the right-hand (western) side of the paved expanse. After traveling beside the paved road, the trail splits; turn left and descend sharply for 0.2 mile. Turn right onto a tote road for a brief walk and then turn right again back onto the narrow blue-blazed trail. Here the trail ascends steeply along a rim of the hill for 0.3 mile. Soon, your feet will begin slipping on the loose, grapefruit-sized rocks lining the path. Ask kids what might make a trail slippery and hard to walk on: loose rocks, wet moss or leaves, pine needles, etc. As you look to the left, the woods open up and an impressive rock slide soon comes into view. Near the crest of West Peak, you must scramble over the upper reaches of this rock slide, which has formed a narrow ravine. Let the kids go first and challenge them to find the surest footing. The Sleeping Giant naps on a lush, green carpet far below. You emerge onto a gravel path at the summit after 3 miles of tough hiking. Turn right onto the path that leads to the parking lot for West Peak. Access the pre- cipitous ledges of West Peak through a gate in the fence that borders the south side of the parking lot. Exercise caution here with the smaller ones but enjoy the dramatic 270-degree views. Return as you came.

17. Chauncey Peak and Lamentation Mountain

Type: Dayhike
Difficulty: Moderate for children
Distance: 4.2 miles, round trip
Hiking time: 4 hours
High point/elevation gain: 720 feet, 650 feet
Hikable: May–October
Maps: USGS Middletown and Meriden

This one will take your breath away—literally, at first, as you pick your way up a steep slope for 0.25 mile and then figuratively as you gaze from atop a rocky outcrop at the distant hills and the towns nestled in the faraway valleys. The vistas are so magnificent they seem almost unreal. It feels as if you are standing on a stage with a spectacular backdrop rather than perching on the edge of a 300-foot cliff. As you inch along the edge of the ridge that rises over Crescent Lake, the breathtaking panoramas continue until the path curls into the woods and heads for Lamentation Mountain. In this case, good judgment is more critical to a successful hike than physical stamina—the only significant vertical gain occurs immediately. Older children with previous hiking experience and the ability to proceed with caution will thoroughly enjoy this trip.

 Take Exit 20 (Country Club Road and Middle Street) off I-91 in Middletown. Travel west on Country Club Road, crossing the Meriden city line and passing a trap rock quarry. Two and two-tenths miles from the highway, notice blue blazes on the telephone poles. At 2.5 miles, just before the road turns sharply left and another road splits off to the right, park on the widened shoulder on the right-hand side of the road.

Light blue rectangular blazes mark the Mattabesett Trail that heads west into the woods up a moderate incline. The climb steepens as you continue, and the way becomes littered with loose stones, turning steps into backward slides. Though this will be a difficult section for kids to navigate, remind them that their efforts will take them to the crest quickly where the trail then leads along relatively level terrain. Approaching the height of the hill, natural rock steps carved in the granite face assist hikers in the final scramble.

At the top, 0.25 mile from the base, the trail turns right and follows along the southeast rim of Chauncey Peak. Here the trail reveals its daring character as it inches along exposed granite, precariously close to the cliffs rising hundreds of feet over scenic central Connecticut. The children will enjoy the same delightful "top-of-the-world" sensation from their safe position well back from the dropoff. A narrow ravine cut into the cliffs on the right will beckon adventurous kids, but the walls drop steeply and parents may have to distract their Tarzans-to-be with promises of more trailside challenges to come.

Beyond this first overlook, the trail begins its western journey along the wooded ridge, heading for the cliffs that rise from Crescent Lake. To the right, a quarry mining operation has eaten into the hillside. Take a right-hand side trail to examine this operation from above. Beyond the quarry path, the Mattabesett

A fallen tree frames a curious young hiker.

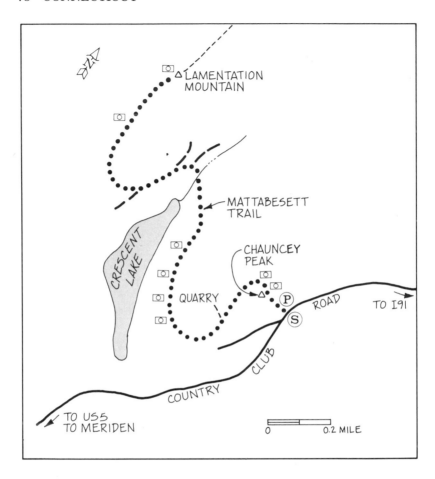

Trail dips and then mounts a section of the ridge at 0.6 mile with impressive views over Crescent Lake to similar ridges across the water and beyond. Soon, the wide trail extends to cliff's edge. You may want to take a lunch break here, since the views are as magnificent as any you will encounter for the remainder of the hike. Consider turning around here if the kids are getting tired— remember, you have a 0.75-mile walk back to your car. As you continue carefully picking your way along the exposed ledge to the lake's northern tip, the trail begins to curl around the head of the lake and then drops steeply through a hemlock forest. Watch for the blue blazes as side trails enter and exit the Mattabesett.

As the trail bottoms out, cross a stream that feeds the lake and follow the footpath as it swerves right and begins the gradual, rocky ascent of Lamentation Mountain. Sections of this trail may swell with water during spring runoff. Soon, the trail bears left away from this sometimes-dormant stream bed, continuing on blue blazes. This ascent, though constant, is not nearly as severe as the climb to Chauncey Peak. The blue-blazed trail intersects with jeep trails and fire roads, at times joining them for a stretch and at other times cutting across them. The kids can help you watch for the frequent blue markings at these junctions to avoid turning off the Mattabesett Trail. Soon the path leaves the crisscrossing jeep trails and narrows, still on a moderate ascent. Lamentation's wooded summit, at 2.1 miles, offers good views of the tower on Castle Crag to the west and the Sleeping Giant to the south. Turn around at the USGS marker that announces the elevation to be 720 feet. Return the way you came carefully.

18. Wadsworth Falls State Park

Type:	Dayhike
Difficulty:	Easy for children
Distance:	3.2 miles, round trip
Hiking time:	2 hours
High point/elevation gain:	210 feet, 240 feet
Hikable:	Year-round
Maps:	USGS Middletown

Waterfalls are a favorite trailside feature for adults as well as kids. On this hike, you'll encounter two of them. Even better, these falls can be enjoyed by the youngest hikers because the route we've chosen is appropriate for everyone. If you visit in the spring, you'll get the full effect of swelled rivers exploding over the cliffs. In the warmer months, you can cool off after your hike with a swim at the pond (located near the park's main entrance). Picnic tables and fireplaces are available for those who want to cook up a post-hike feast.

From CT-66 in Middletown, take CT-157 South (Wadsworth Street), following signs to Wadsworth Falls in Middlefield. You'll reach the park entrance on the left in 1.5 miles; turn here. You will have to pay a moderate parking fee on summer weekends.

The well-marked Main Trail starts to the left of the parking

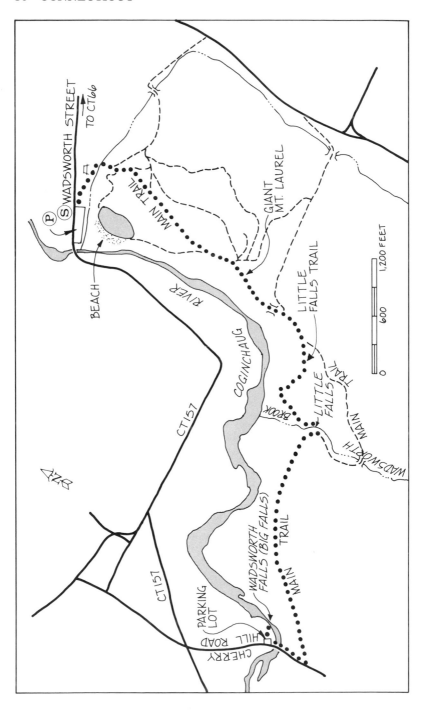

Big Falls at Wadsworth Falls State Park

area (as you face the pond) behind the picnic area and horseshoe
pits. This wide, clay path, blazed infrequently with orange marks,
is crisscrossed by numerous other trails; be sure to stick to the orange blazes of the Main Trail. Shortly, a sign shows the way to
Big Falls, 1.6 miles away. Can you hear the chattering of the red
squirrels? One-half mile from the start, a sign points out the colony of giant mountain laurel bordering the path. Stop for a rest
on the bench near the park's trail map. How well can the kids
read a trail map? Ask them how far it is to the falls and how far
you have already come. Even a little child can trace the route
with a finger. Then see if anyone wants to guess how much time it

will take to reach the falls based on how long it has taken to get to this point.

Continue along the well-trodden path to a stone bridge over a frequently dry stream bed. At an intersection 0.7 mile from the start, the orange-blazed trail swerves left, but take the right-hand path marked in blue to Little Falls. In 0.2 mile, this narrow, rugged path plummets into a ravine at the base of the falls. Wadsworth Brook tumbles over the rocks in a 30-foot drop, rejuvenating sweaty hikers with a cool misty spray. The blue-blazed Little Falls Trail climbs steeply away from the falls, quickly rejoining the Main Trail. Turn right, following the orange blazes once more on a mild descent along a stream.

Nearly 1.5 miles from the start, the trail outlets on paved Cherry Hill Road. Turn right and walk on the road to another Wadsworth Falls parking area on the right side of the road. (If you leave a second car here, you will avoid the return trip, cutting the total hiking distance in half. Another variation on this trip would be to park here and hike from Wadsworth Falls to Little Falls and back; a 1.4-mile total.) Follow the path that heads out of the parking area—the children will lead the way, following the sound of the pounding water to its source. The Coginchaug River bursts over a rim of rocks 100 feet wide and plunges 25 feet, creating a miniature Niagara Falls. With fences bordering the riverbank at the top of Wadsworth Falls, older children may be able to do some exploring on their own. Enjoy the mesmerizing sights and sounds of this dramatic waterfall from above and below before heading back to your car along the familiar Main Trail.

19. Coginchaug Cave

Type: Dayhike
Difficulty: Easy for children
Distance: 2.2 miles, round trip
Hiking time: 1.5 hours
High point/elevation gain: 540 feet, 240 feet
Hikable: April–November
Maps: USGS Durham

Kids and caves go together like cookies and milk. Coginchaug Cave, along the Mattabesett Trail, rises 30 feet high and stretches more than 50 feet along the base of a cliff. It is said to have provided shelter to Indians long ago. One of the children might even come across a primitive Indian tool here; other hikers have. Take this relatively short, easy walk to the cave on an overcast day, saving the sunnier days for those hikes that promise long-range views.

From the junction of CT-17 and CT-79 in Durham center, drive south on CT-79 for 0.8 mile. Turn left (east) on Old Blue Hills Road following blue blazes on telephone poles. Continue along this road for a short distance to its cul-de-sac conclusion and park on the right-hand side.

Follow the driveway that continues beyond the cul-de-sac turnaround. The blue blazes will lead you straight into the woods at the junction of two driveways. Initially, the blazes are sparse as you follow along a jeep road bordered by utility lines. At about 0.3 mile, after a short ascent and some level walking, the trail turns right onto another jeep trail through denser woods. At 0.5 mile, bear left at a second intersection, still on the blue blazes.

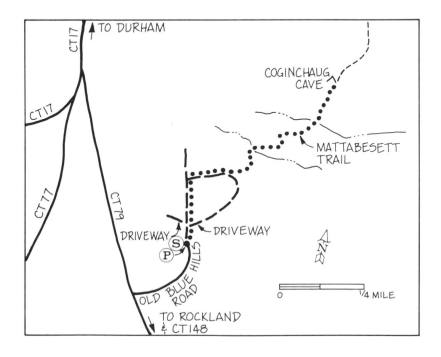

The trail winds through a thickly wooded area, past rock outcrop-pings, and then crosses a small stream. Have the children count how many stones they must step on in order to get across.

After several short climbs and descents, the blazes take you across another brook. At the 1-mile mark, a final sharp ascent brings hikers through a colony of mountain laurel. Almost imme-diately, a tricky descent sweeps left along the belly of the ridge to the cave. Give younger children a hand here. Coginchaug Cave is an impressive rock overhang that faces east; it is best to do your exploring in the morning with the sun over your shoulder. Ask

What do mushrooms feel like?

the kids what it must have been like for the Indians who used this cave as their home. What did they eat? What did they sleep on? Did the Indian children play games on the rocks and cliffs near the cave? Return via the blue trail to your car.

20. Bluff Head on Totoket Mountain

Type: Dayhike
Difficulty: Moderate for children
Distance: 2.5 miles, round trip
Hiking time: 2 hours
High point/elevation gain: 720 feet, 400 feet
Hikable: March–November
Maps: USGS Durham

Don your sturdy hiking boots, pack a pair of binoculars, and head for Totoket Mountain's Bluff Head on a bright, clear day. Much of this trail flirts with the edge of the steep cliff, affording dizzying views but creating problems for those with curious, eager little hikers. Due to the initial steep climb (you will gain about 200 feet within the first 500 feet of trail) and the nature of the trail, this hike is best suited for preteens who will appreciate the panoramas and will exercise caution atop the numerous outlooks.

From I-95 in Guilford take Exit 58 and travel north on CT- 77. At the junction of CT-77 and CT-80 in Guilford, drive 4.2 miles north on CT-77 to an off-road parking area on the left.

The blue-blazed Mattabesett Trail heads west from the parking area up a very steep, wide trail. On this initial ascent, the trail is heavily eroded; loose soil and shale rocks make for tough going. Kids will need lots of encouragement. Soon this challenging terrain gives way to more gradual climbing on a hard-packed, heavily wooded trail. As you travel along the eastern edge of the Totoket Mountain ridge, you may catch a glimpse of the vistas across the valley to your right. Within the first 0.5 mile, you will arrive at an overlook with a fine easterly view across farmlands

Father and son return from Bluff Head.

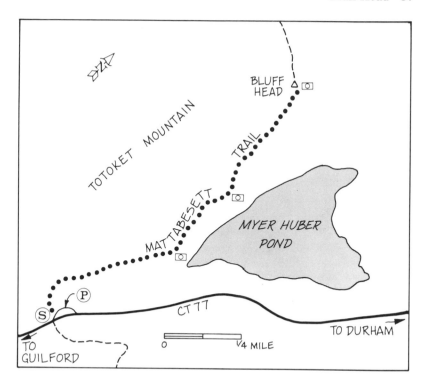

and forests. Children should be reminded to stay back from the
edge of this cliff, which drops straight down for 150 feet. Give
your young companions the binoculars so that they can watch the
distant cows grazing or the farmer haying his faraway field.

The trail plunges back into the woods, then returns to the
edge of the ridge, repeating this pattern several times within the
next 0.75 mile. At the second overlook, Myer Huber Pond is visible to your left (northeast). Before you arrive at the final overlook, a short descent into the woods is followed by a sharp ascent
that leads to the top of Bluff Head. Near the crest, a dramatic,
narrow ravine drops to the base of this cliff. Children will be able
to imagine Tarzan sailing across this chasm wrapped around a
jungle vine.

At a rock outcropping close to the top of Bluff Head, a footpath curls around the rock's right-hand side. Triple blue blazes
indicate, however, that this is not the recommended route because the path travels very closely along the edge of the cliff.
Instead, follow the trail that heads through the middle of the out-

cropping to the top of Bluff Head. From here, the earth appears to fall away at your feet and you are rewarded with stunning views of the seemingly miniature pond and rural countryside. Though it may seem miles away, the Myer Huber Pond is actually about 500 feet below you. After the kids have rested and enjoyed a snack, return the way you came, exercising caution on the final, steep descent near the parking area.

21. Chatfield Hollow State Park

Type: Dayhike
Difficulty: Easy for children
Distance: 2.5 miles, loop
Hiking time: 2 hours
High point/elevation gain: 385 feet, 250 feet
Hikable: May–September
Maps: USGS Clinton

On a warm summer day, the beach and swimming area at Schreeder Pond teem with activity. Parking spots are tough to come by and picnic tables are filled as quickly as they are vacated. But the 18 miles of trails that wind through the surrounding woods are yours alone. Long ago, Indians hunted and fished in this valley. The many Indian artifacts that have been found here indicate that the natives slept beneath the rock overhangs and held tribal meetings in the rocky hills. Kids may be lucky enough to find an arrowhead. It's unlikely, though, that they will come across any signs of the witches said to have inhabited the area. Legends tell of the two mischievous witches, "Goody Wee" and "Betty Wee," who lived in the hollow and enjoyed playing nasty tricks on their neighbors.

   Take Exit 63 off of I-95. Travel north 5.1 miles on CT-81 to a rotary that joins CT-80. Drive west on CT-80 in Killingworth for 1.2 miles to the Chatfield Hollow State Park entrance on the right. Turn here. (Pay a moderate parking fee.) In 0.2 mile, you will pass the well-marked "Look Out Trail" trailhead on the right. Continue on the paved park road to the parking spaces near the Schreeder Pond beach.

Post-hike sunbathing and storytelling at Schreeder Pond

Walk along the park road heading back toward the entrance. At the junction with Look Out Trail (about 0.2 mile), turn left. Within the first 100 yards, the white-blazed trail splits; follow the right-hand branch. The rocky, rugged trail ascends gradually for 0.3 mile, leading hikers over a series of ups and downs; it crosses a stream and runs alongside stone walls and a huge granite outcropping on the left. The children might want to pause and touch the bark on the different kinds of trees: How does the bark on a pine tree feel different from the bark on a birch tree? As you begin to hear the sounds of a stream, a side trail branches off on the right. Ignore the side trail and continue straight to a junction with the blue-blazed East Woods Trail at 0.5 mile. Here, turn left, remaining on the white-blazed Look Out Trail that heads up to the top of a ridge with good local views. Beyond the ridge, the trail descends, curling to the right, then climbs again to the top of another unexposed ridge.

After traversing more rolling terrain and passing a distinc-

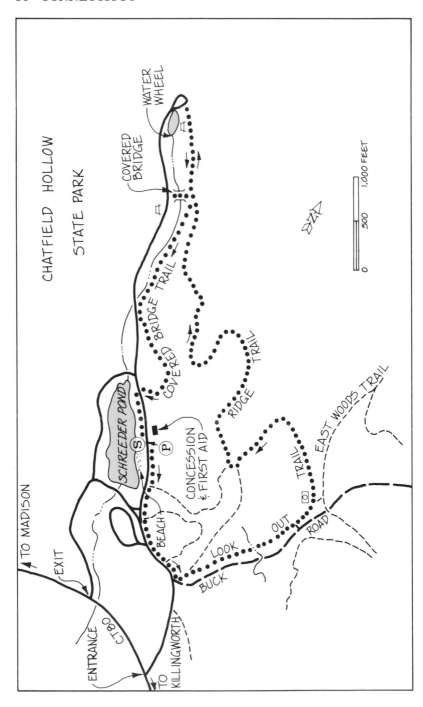

CHATFIELD HOLLOW
STATE PARK

tive rock formation on the right, you will arrive at a fork in another 0.3 mile. To the left, the white-blazed Look Out Trail wanders back to the park road. Take the right-hand unblazed path and in 50 feet, turn right onto the red-blazed Ridge Trail. This trail, rugged and rough, is similar in character to the Look Out Trail. Take turns choosing categories such as birds, tree stumps, and mushrooms and count how many of each you see along the way. Soon, you will arrive at the top of a rock ridge with 30- to 40-foot dropoffs to the left. Can the kids hear the noisy crowds on Schreeder Pond's beach? Soon they will be able to take a dip too. The trail bends right into the woods away from the crowds over a series of easy (but tiring) ups and downs. Near the end of the Ridge Trail, be sure to stay on the path marked by red blazes. The path eventually reaches the Covered Bridge Trail; bear right for now and follow the Ridge Trail to its conclusion 1.8 miles from the start of the hike. Here, near a small pond with a water wheel at its outlet, picnic tables provide a good spot for a lunch break.

After your snack, return on the Ridge Trail to the junction with the Covered Bridge Trail. Turn right to admire the covered bridge spanning the river (more picnic tables offer an alternative lunch spot). Return to the Covered Bridge/Ridge Trail intersection and turn right on the Covered Bridge Trail, marked with purple blazes. This trail is reasonably flat, with rock ledges bordering the left side and a river on the right. The trail briefly exits onto the park road, immediately turning hard left back into the woods on an ascent. At the height of this trail, the blazes lead along some 12-foot-high cliffs. Hikers slip through a split boulder and then begin the final descent. The trail drops more steeply as it approaches the park road with well-placed rocks to assist you on your descent. At the outlet to the park road, 2.3 miles from the start of the hike, turn left and follow the road back to your car. You've earned a swim.

22. Westwoods Preserve

Type: Dayhike
Difficulty: Difficult for children
Distance: 3.2 miles, round trip
Hiking time: 4 hours
High point/elevation gain: 150 feet, 450 feet
Hikable: April–November
Maps: USGS Guilford

You can't judge a trail by the trailhead. In this case, the innocent-looking path that leads from the parking area quickly becomes a trail that commands hikers to scale steep and rugged granite walls, crawl through stone passageways, and inch across sloping rock faces. The trails wander through the 2000-acre preserve for 40 miles, marked with an intricate blazing system in which shapes as well as colors differentiate the trails. Paths crisscross one another and a trail may come within yards of intersecting a previously traversed section. It's easy to get confused. Pre-teens who are experienced hikers will handily meet the challenges of Westwoods and brag to school chums about their day spent imitating Indiana Jones. But younger kids and even adults without much experience should opt for something a little easier.

From New Haven, drive east on I-95 North for 11 miles to Exit 57. Turn right (southeast) onto US 1 (Boston Post Road) heading toward Guilford. In 0.5 mile, turn right onto Peddlers Road. (Trail maps are available at Bishop's Orchards, which is on the left-hand side of US 1, just beyond Peddlers Road.) Drive 1 mile to a small driveway/parking lot on the left, just past Denison Drive.

The trail marked with white circles and occasional white rectangles begins as a continuation of the driveway on a paved path. Be sure to differentiate among the various shapes as well as colors of blazes. Soon, at double white circle blazes, the circle trail splits off left while the rectangles continue straight. Follow the circle trail on a descent through a colony of mountain laurel bushes. In June, the prolific pink and white blossoms reveal why the mountain laurel was chosen as Connecticut's state flower. A green trail veers left and soon the white rectangle trail rejoins

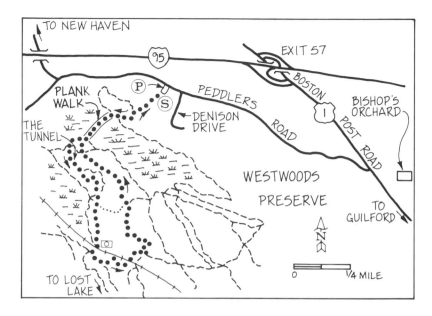

from the right; at all junctions, follow white circles. The trail crosses a swamp on a narrow, overgrown plank walk for almost 0.1 mile. Children will feel as if they are taking a brief trip through the jungle as they push back the thick vegetation on either side. At the edge of the marsh, a yellow trail veers right, an orange trail heads left, and the white trail continues straight. Follow the yellow circle trail to the right. After quickly ascending a rocky ridge through more mountain laurel bushes, you will notice numerous so-called "crossover" trails splitting from the yellow circle trail. Watch carefully for the yellow circle blazes that will mark most of your route. Just beyond one of the many crossover trail intersections at the 0.6-mile mark, the trail curls to the left and plunges through a 40-foot-long rock tunnel. Near the passageway's narrow end, only crawling and squeezing will return you to daylight. (The kids may insist on a repeat of the tunnel!) Once outside the passageway, the trail turns right, following below the granite mass that houses the lengthy cave.

   In the next 0.5 mile, the trail snakes over and under 30- to 50-foot rock cliffs and, again, more side trails split off to the left and right. The tremendous rock outcroppings that appear on your left at first will inch closer and closer until soon you will be climbing through a narrow ridge traversing those very rocks. After making your way across the rock face, follow the trail as it switches back right and climbs to the top of the cliff. Again the trail drops to the bottom of the cliffs and rises to another crest. Children (and their parents) will not have time to worry about blisters because this trail presents challenge after thrilling challenge from start to finish. Soon, you will pass an area where ice has exerted its force and created fissures in the rock. (A left-hand turn onto a green blazed trail at approximately 1 mile will bring you to to an intersection with a white-blazed trail 0.15 mile later. Turn left again and in 0.5 mile you will be back at the swamp crossing. Continue to the parking area for a 2-mile total hike.)

If you opt to continue, you will ascend another series of ridges just beyond the intersection with the green-blazed trail. At one point, you will be forced to scoot across a sloping cliff on your butt because a rock overhang makes standing impossible. As the trail winds through forest dominated by hemlocks, kids will get a kick out of the frequent squeezes through rock passageways. After approximately 1.3 miles, you will arrive atop a rock dome with pretty, southerly views of an adjoining ridge. Utility wires stretch across the valley below. Continue to follow the yellow circle blazes that lead hikers along the edge of the dome. Double switch-backs along a narrow path trimmed in mountain laurel lead you down the side of the dome facing the power lines. To your left, the ridge drops precipitously. At the bottom of this ridge, the trail emerges left on an overgrown path that crosses under the utility lines. Just beyond the power lines, the yellow-blazed trail branches off to the right on a muddy path and continues to Lost Lake. At this intersection (where the blazing may be indistinct), you turn left on a blue-blazed jeep trail. The next intersection is marked with numerous blazes; bear left here, still on a jeep trail, and cross back under the power lines. At the next intersection, stay straight on blue blazes. Within 100 feet, the blue- and white-blazed trails split. Bear left toward the white circular blazes and follow them for the remainder of the hike. After a series of additional climbs over rugged terrain (at times, children will need guidance), the trail levels off. Head straight through an intersection with the green-blazed trail. As you cross a patch of exposed granite, you will begin to hear sounds from the highway. At 2.75 miles from the start, you will cross back over the wetlands along the plank walk and soon reach the parking area and your car.

Right out of The Jungle Book—*overgrown boardwalk in Westwoods Preserve*

23. Gillette Castle State Park

Type: Dayhike
Difficulty: Easy for children
Distance: 1.3 miles, round trip
Hiking time: 1 hour
High point/elevation gain: 185 feet, 220 feet
Hikable: May–December
Maps: USGS Deep River

If your children thrill to stories of Cinderella or Sleeping Beauty, they will be enchanted by the storybook quality of Gillette Castle and the riverside grounds. The ivy-covered castle perches atop the seventh of the Seven Sisters hills that border the Connecticut River. William Gillette, a Connecticut native and well-known stage actor at the turn of the century, designed every detail of his 24-room dream house. Since one of his great fascinations was trains, he constructed a railroad that left a depot at the castle's front door and meandered through the forest to the eastern end of the property. Gillette was understandably concerned about the future of this magnificent estate and in his will he ordered his heirs to "see to it that the property did not fall into the hands of some blithering saphead" who wouldn't recognize its value. Certainly all who visit today appreciate Gillette's efforts and vision. Some folks like to come in September and October, when the surrounding hills blush with autumn color. Others make it a tradition to visit at Christmastime when the castle rooms are gaily decorated in holiday reds and greens. Encourage the grandparents to take the children on this hike. It's perfect for the oldest and youngest members of the family.

 At the junction of CT-148 and CT-82 near the village of Hadlyme (in Lyme), travel west on CT-148 for 1.6 miles. Turn right onto River Road (unmarked, just east of the Connecticut River). Travel 0.7 mile on River Road to the park entrance on the left. Go to the end of the park road and leave your car in the parking lot.

Stroll up the paved path to the castle, passing the manicured lawns decorated with fountains and statues. From the impeccably detailed stone patio overlooking the Connecticut River, head right (northwest) to Grand Central Station, the main terminal for the now-dismantled Seventh Sister Shortline. This open-sided, stone veranda is one of the loveliest picnic spots you'll ever find. Below the station on the river side, a sign for the Loop Trail and river vistas indicates a 0.5-mile route. Head northwesterly along this Loop Trail counterclockwise, away from the crowded castle lawn. Magnificent footbridges and stone turrets punctuate the worn path that descends gently to a plateau near the riverbank. At the far reaches of this trail, near the water, the path switches back along a rocky ledge. Here, the bordering fence is missing, so take the children's hands. The path never dips right to the water's

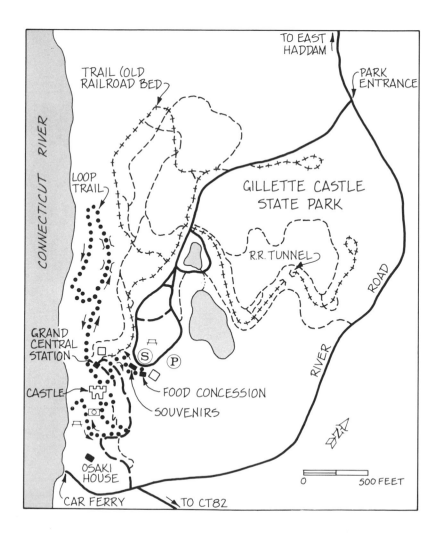

The Gillette Castle grounds

edge because the state's Department of Enviromental Protection has decided to protect this delicate area from further erosion. Instead, the trail climbs back through an evergreen forest to the head of the loop trail and the castle.

From the castle patio (facing the river), head left down a flight of stairs and walk into the woods on a footpath. The trail wanders through the forest to a point of land on a ledge (bordered with a fence) high above the river. Enjoy stunning water views from the overlook and then follow the trail to the left. In 0.1 mile, the path joins a gravel road; turn right. In another 0.1 mile, turn right onto a wide path that departs the road, descending along the edge of the ridge to the Connecticut River. Relax on the grass near a small beach where visitors picnic and others have set up camp. The kids can wade and watch the boats. Reverse direction to return to the castle. You may decide to explore some of the other paths or, for a small admission price, you can peek at the inside of the castle before returning to your car.

Notes: Park hours are daily, 8:00 a.m. to sunset. The castle is open Memorial Day through Columbus Day, 10:00 a.m. to 5:00 p.m. From Columbus Day to the last weekend before Christmas, it is open weekends only from 10:00 a.m. to 4:00 p.m. There is a small admission fee for the castle for ages 6 and over.

24. Devil's Hopyard State Park

Type: Dayhike or overnight
Difficulty: Easy for children
Distance: 2.6 miles, loop
Hiking time: 2 hours
High point/elevation gain: 480 feet, 380 feet
Hikable: Year-round
Maps: USGS Hamburg

Ask a dozen locals how this park got its name and you'll hear a dozen different tales. One legend claims that the numerous potholes at the base of Chapman Falls were created when the devil hopped with his hot hooves from one ledge to another, trying not to get wet. (Actually, the potholes were created as stones moving downstream became trapped in an eddy and spun around until a crater formed in the rock.) A less intriguing story claims that a farmer named Dibble grew hops in the area, and Dibble's Hopyard eventually came to be called Devil's Hopyard. No matter how the name originated, the 860-acre Devil's Hopyard State Park draws a multitude of visitors each summer who come to enjoy the pleasant picnic areas along the bank of the Eight Mile River and the 15 miles of hiking trails. Chapman Falls, at the northern end of the park, seems to attract the most attention from visitors. Here, the Eight Mile River crashes 60 feet over the rock escarpment to the calm pool below. A camping area near the falls provides overnighters with a choice of more than 20 open and wooded sites.

 From I-395 in Waterford take Exit 2 onto CT-85 North. In 7.5 miles, turn left onto CT-82 West. (A sign points the way to Devil's Hopyard and Gillette Castle.) Drive 4.7 miles on CT-82 to Hopyard Road; turn right. In 3.0 miles, enter the parking area on your right.

The hike begins at the covered bridge spanning the Eight Mile River. Cross over the river and turn left, following the orange rectangular-blazed Vista Trail. Bear right at the first trail intersection. At triple orange blazes, after a stream crossing over a footbridge, turn right, following a "To Vista" sign. This rugged, root-crossed trail initially climbs along a meager tributary to the Eight Mile River, going straight (east) as side trails split left. Cross the stream at 0.25 mile on a jumble of rocks (in the spring, wet feet are guaranteed). At an intersection with a white-blazed trail, continue straight, still ascending moderately along orange blazes. The path departs the stream and descends through a stand of hemlocks, entering another wet area on rolling terrain. The kids will have to pick their way across several more streams before reaching an intersection at 1.3 miles where the orange trail goes right. Follow the side trail (left), marked with an occasional orange blaze, that ends at an overlook. Here, hikers are treated to magnificent views to the south of the bucolic Eight Mile River valley.

Follow this short side trail as it drops to the exposed ledges—a great spot for a snack. Because the ledges descend in a series of tiers before the final steep dropoff, parents can relax and concentrate on the vistas with the children on the upper ledges. Return

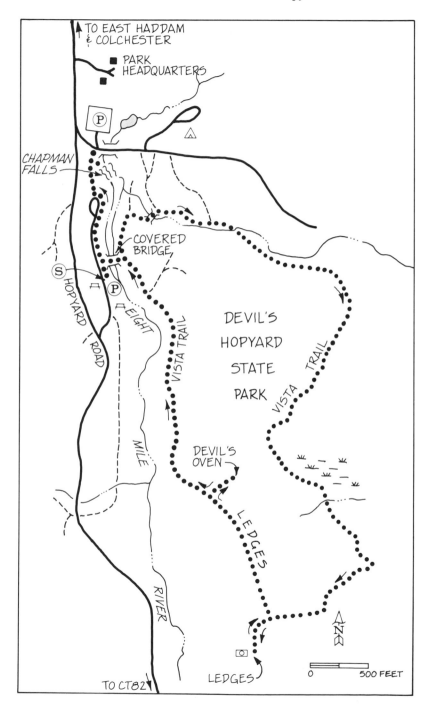

TO EAST HADDAM & COLCHESTER

PARK HEADQUARTERS

CHAPMAN FALLS

COVERED BRIDGE

S

HOPYARD ROAD

EIGHT MILE RIVER

VISTA TRAIL

DEVIL'S HOPYARD STATE PARK

VISTA TRAIL

DEVIL'S OVEN

LEDGES

LEDGES

N

0   500 FEET

TO CT 82

to the intersection, turning left onto the orange-blazed trail to continue the loop. The path drops moderately beside overhanging rock ledges on the right, then swings closer to the Eight Mile River. At 1.7 miles, a large yellow arrow points to the right. Follow this side trail up a short, steep ascent to a rock outcropping that harbors a small cave called the Devil's Oven.

Postcard-perfect Chapman Falls

After the kids have had a chance to explore, pick your way back down the slope to the main trail and turn right as the path continues to follow the river upstream. As the trail flirts with the river's edge, it becomes more rugged with lots of stumbling potential for tired little legs. After a final brief but steep uphill climb, the trail drops along a wide gravel road. In another 0.3 mile, the blue-blazed loop trail joins from the right and in 0.1 mile you return to the covered bridge for a 2.2-mile total.

With your car in sight, it might be tempting to head toward the parking lot but instead turn right after you cross the bridge en route to Chapman Falls. (It's worth it—we promise.) Follow the paved park road past the parking spaces to a wide gravel path that soon arrives at the falls. Admire the waterfall from above and then drop to the bottom on a side trail where smooth rocks near the pool provide a great place to do some deep thinking. Best of all, the sound of the cascading water is guaranteed to drown out whining. When you're sufficiently relaxed, return to your car.

25. Rocky Neck State Park

Type: Dayhike or overnight
Difficulty: Easy for children
Distance: 3.5 miles, loop
Hiking time: 2.5 hours
High point/elevation gain: 50 feet, 100 feet
Hikable: Year-round
Maps: USGS Old Lyme

In the heat of a summer day, hiking the tame Four Mile River Trail to the beach can be a great way to combine hiking with swimming, wading, or sunbathing. Even in cooler weather, Rocky Neck's seashore can be enjoyed for the distinct pleasures it offers your senses. In the spring, watch at the estuary as the fresh water from Four Mile River rushes to meet the salty ocean water of Long Island Sound. Look at the cranes and herons wandering among the cattails in autumn. See the fishermen reeling in striped bass, flounder, or mackerel in the early dawn, or at dusk.

Looking over the tidal flat from Tony's Nose

In winter, smell the sharp, salty breeze. But do be careful—this is the area where Lyme Disease got its name. Be sure to follow the appropriate recommendations detailed in the introduction. Campsites at Rocky Neck are within walking distance of the beach at the eastern edge of the park.

  From the Connecticut Turnpike (I-95) in East Lyme, take Exit 72, following the signs to Rocky Neck State Park. Drive south for 0.5 mile to the junction with CT-156. Though the Rocky Neck signs indicate a left-hand turn, go right instead onto CT-156. In 0.6 mile, park on the right just before the bridge over the Four Mile River and the East Lyme/Old Lyme town line.

The trail, indicated by stakes painted white or white with yellow arrows, starts on the eastern side of Four Mile River. Follow the white-blazed Four Mile River Trail along a wide, grassy path through an open field and into the woods up a small hill. When the yellow trail bears left, stay to the right on a path that will eventually take you to the pavilion. At 0.8 mile, bear right on a blue side trail to an overlook called Tony's Nose. Here, rocky ledges rise 40 feet above the river and offer excellent views over the tidal flat. Return to the main trail, bearing right at all intersections and soon merge with a paved road. Bear right beyond a small parking area. The road travels over railroad tracks by way

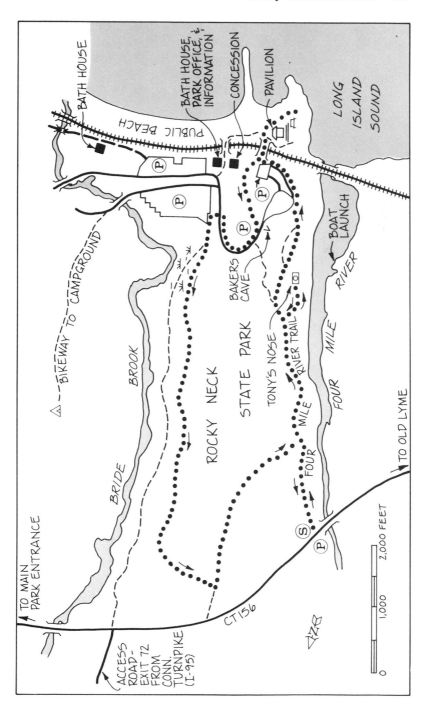

of an arched bridge and emerges onto the pavilion grounds 1 mile from the start. Ask kids to compare the man-made railroad bed with Mother Nature's sand dunes. What do they have in common? (Both serve to protect the inland areas from the storms and fierce winds blowing in off the ocean.) As you face the lovely ocean views, a crowded beach is to your left; to the right is a private, wooded area overlooking Rocky Neck, a perfect picnic spot. Stop here if you are not planning to relax at the public beach.

To continue your hike, head back across the bridge and bear right on a gravel road. Head left through a grassy parking area and then turn right on the paved park road. The kids can try to find Baker's Cave, a rock overhang on the left-hand side of the road. The cave was named for a man who hid there during the Revolutionary War to avoid serving in the army. His family brought him food and supplies at night; he was never discovered. Follow the park road to a large parking lot where a footpath plunges back into the woods on the left, approximately 150 feet from the road. When the path divides in 0.1 mile, bear left on a trail that skirts a marsh frequented by nesting osprey. After another mile of pleasant woods walking, turn left (south) at a trail junction onto a yellow-blazed trail and in 0.4 mile turn right (north) onto the white-blazed Four Mile River Trail. In 0.2 mile, you will arrive at your car.

26. Bluff Point State Park

Type:	Dayhike
Difficulty:	Moderate for children
Distance:	6 miles, loop (including sand spit)
Hiking time:	4.5 hours
High point/elevation gain:	100 feet, 140 feet
Hikable:	Year-round
Maps:	USGS New London

It's hard to find a stretch of Connecticut seashore that is not overrun with condominiums, dockside boutiques, or waterfront industry. But a 780-acre tract of land known as Bluff Point offers a refuge from the crowded consequences of overdevelopment. Here, the kids can scale lofty bluffs, hike through delightful oceanside forests, and run along a sand spit that stretches half a mile into the bay. They can watch scaups, or diving ducks, plunge for crabs or barnacles and scan the water for swans or mallards. At hike's end, weary walkers can take a dip at the small stretch of beach set aside for swimmers. For an afternoon, the kids can enjoy the ocean the way their great-grandparents did.

From I-95 in Groton, take Exit 88 to CT-117 ("Groton, Long Point"). Turn right (south) onto CT-117. After 1 mile, turn right (west) at a T intersection with US 1 (US 1 not indicated). Drive 0.3 mile to the first traffic light (the Groton Town Hall is on the left). Turn left here onto Depot Road and drive 0.4 mile. Bear right under a railroad bridge where the paved road gives way to gravel. In another 0.3 mile, you will arrive at a parking area for visitors to Bluff Point. The park is open from 8:00 a.m. to sunset.

Walk along the gravel road, passing through the barricade for motor vehicles. For the first 0.4 mile or so, the road follows the shoreline—you might decide to wander along the sandy beach instead of sticking to the path. On the shore, you will encounter a few sunbathers and clam diggers if the weather is warm. The kids may want to pause and get an up-close look at clamming. At approximately the 0.6-mile mark, the road breaks left from the beach and travels over a wooded knoll. Ocean scents and distant sights remind everyone that this is no ordinary woods walk. At approximately 0.9 mile, on the down side of a brief grade, are rustic rest facilities. Beyond this point, the road drops and then crests another bluff where a walking path veers right and runs along a rocky ridge overlooking Long Island Sound. This is the hike's most scenic spot and the best place for a picnic or merely a rest. Kids can count sailboats while the bigger folks scan the skies for terns and tree swallows. Drop to the shore and follow it to the sand spit that reaches into the bay. (Eliminating the sand spit section of the hike will make the total mileage 3.7 miles.) Along the center of the spit, dunes sculpted by the wind and waves shelter nesting sandpipers.

After exploring this narrow strip of sand and beach grass, return to the main trail, bearing right at trail junctions to remain close to the boulder beach. At the point's easternmost tip, a massive boulder guards the beach, worn on its seaward side from the relentless pounding of the waves. The coastal path eventually

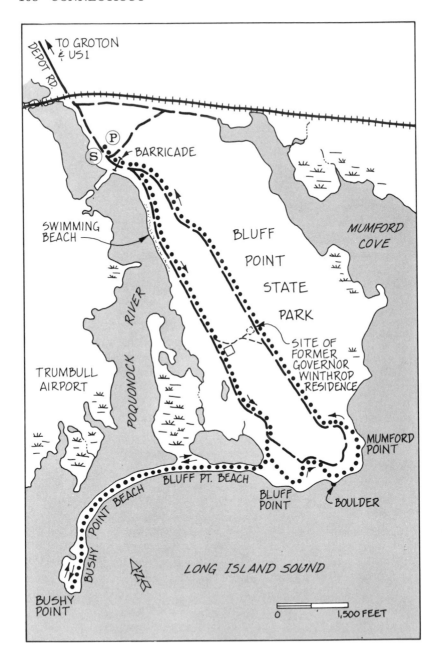

TO GROTON
& US1

DEPOT RD.

BARRICADE

P

S

SWIMMING
BEACH

BLUFF

POINT

STATE

PARK

MUMFORD
COVE

POQUONOCK RIVER

TRUMBULL
AIRPORT

SITE OF
FORMER
GOVERNOR
WINTHROP
RESIDENCE

MUMFORD
POINT

BLUFF PT. BEACH

BUSHY POINT BEACH

BLUFF
POINT

BOULDER

BUSHY
POINT

LONG ISLAND SOUND

0   1,500 FEET

leads hikers back to the main road. If you ventured to the far reaches of the sand spit, you have walked 4.5 miles to this point. You will follow this park road in a northerly direction for another 1.4 miles, traveling through a surprisingly dense forest that is home to a large number of white-tailed deer. Challenge the kids to find evidence of these majestic animals that frequently gather at the forest's edge. Look for twigs and buds that have been chewed off and trunks that have been stripped of bark. Shortly before you arrive at the parking area, you join the original gravel road. Let the children take a plunge into the water before you begin the trip home.

27. Narragansett Trail to High Ledge Lookout

Type: Daytrip
Difficulty: Moderate for children
Distance: 4.2 miles, round trip
Hiking time: 3 hours
High point/elevation gain: 512 feet, 220 feet
Hikable: April–October
Maps: USGS Old Mystic

This is a gratifying hike for all members of the family with some rocky climbs to challenge the veteran hikers and easy woods walking for the smaller guys. High Ledge Lookout, three-quarters of a mile into the hike, offers pretty views of Wyassup Lake and distant towns, a pleasant setting for a picnic lunch and also a suitable turnaround point. Those wishing to hike the full distance can continue to Bullet Ledge where kids will love exploring the cavelike rock overhangs. It's best not to hike here in late autumn and winter because hunting is permitted then.

Drive to North Stonington Village in southeastern Connecticut, just off CT-2. From the Town Hall and Village Hardware Store, take Wyassup Road (also called Wyassup Lake Road) north for 3 miles to an unmarked road on the left (0.3 mile after Arbor Acres Farm). Turn left and drive 0.7 mile to the boat launch and parking area at Wyassup Lake.

The blue-blazed Narragansett Trail travels the paved road for a short distance before turning left (walk around the gate) onto a wooded road. After nearly 0.2 mile, the trail bears right onto a wide path and soon (less than 0.1 mile) diverges into the woods on the left at the double blue blazes. Imagine the effort and skill that went into fitting together the flat-rock stone wall that borders the right side of the trail at the 0.4-mile mark. The trail quickly turns and rises onto a knoll and then descends into a wet area. After winding through a maze of swampy patches and streams, the path climbs steeply for 0.1 mile. As the path levels off, you will notice another stone wall; in the sections where the stones have not toppled over, the wall is nearly 6 feet high. At 0.7 mile into the hike, you will reach High Ledge Lookout, boasting fine distant views and interesting rock formations. Take a rest

stop. Adults may want to take a few pictures while the kids
scramble over the boulders and duck under the overhangs.

Beyond the lookout, after a steep descent and mirror-image
ascent, more wandering stone walls and unusual rocks keep the
trail from becoming monotonous. A double-blazed left-hand turn
at close to 0.8 mile precedes comfortable rolling terrain. Rhododendron and mountain laurel bushes abound. As the trail follows
a ridge with occasional easterly views, keep young children from
wandering off the trail toward dropoffs. You will come upon a
woods road at 1.3 miles where double blazes indicate a right-hand
turn onto the road. The trail follows the road for 0.4 mile; another
set of double blazes directs hikers to bear left at a fork in the road.
Children can romp ahead on this rolling stretch of road, racing
around the descending switchback at the 1.8-mile mark, staying
on what is clearly the main road and avoiding the side road on the
left. At 2 miles, the trail turns left off the road and curls right

Atop High Ledge Lookout

around Bullet Ledge. The stratified ledges achieve a vertical drop of 40 feet in sections. Children will enjoy exploring the area close to the ledges with rock overhangs forming shallow caves. It's possible to walk around the ledges to access the top of Bullet Ledge, but you will want to accompany your kids to lend a hand. Have a picnic lunch before retracing your steps to the car.

28. Rock Spring Wildlife Refuge

Type:	Dayhike
Difficulty:	Easy for children
Distance:	3.3 miles, loop
Hiking time:	2.25 hours
High point/elevation gain:	500 feet, 310 feet
Hikable:	April–November
Maps:	USGS Scotland

Pile the kids in the car, pick up the grandparents on the way, and head to the 436-acre Rock Spring Wildlife Refuge in Scotland for a hike all members of the family will enjoy. Along the smooth trail with gentle ups and downs, younger children can run ahead without parents worrying about them tripping over rocks or roots. As the trail cuts through a pine plantation, kids will be amazed at the giant trees lined up like soldiers along each side of the trail. The long stretch along river's edge offers abundant examples of busy beavers at work. And just beyond the river, a side trail takes hikers to an outlook with outstanding views of Little River Valley. Best of all—some locals don't even know about this one, so chances are you'll have the place all to yourselves!

 From I-395 in Plainfield, take Exit 89. Drive west on CT-14 approximately 10 miles to CT-97 (Pudding Hill Road), 0.7 mile past the Scotland town line. Travel 1.5 miles north on CT-97 to the preserve on the right-hand side of the street, marked with a 12-foot-high wooden sign (somewhat camouflaged). Park off the road near the trailhead.

Follow the white-blazed trail east, straight into the woods. (This trail is frequented by horseback riders; watch out for manure.) At the display board just 75 feet from the road, sign in and pick up a trail map if one is available. As you continue on the well-worn path through the woods, note the numerous flat stone walls that crisscross the property, indicating that this was once agricultural land. At 0.2 mile, double switchbacks take you to a short, rather steep descent. In the winter, the woods feel spacious and open since oak and maples abound with very few evergreens.

At 0.4 mile, signs at a trail junction offer several options; you should follow the sign for the spring, heading right (south). Pass-

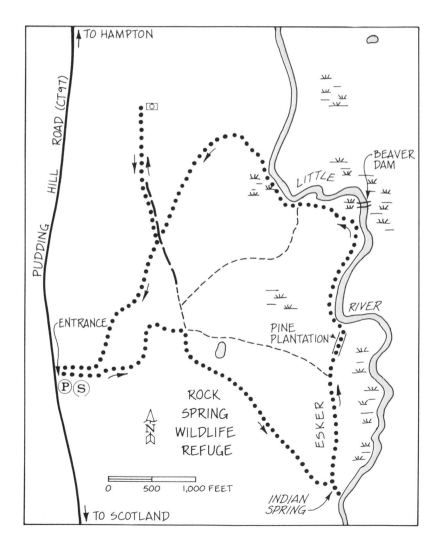

Marching through the pine plantation at Rock Spring Wildlife Refuge

ing some distance from a small pond and through overgrown meadows and a pine thicket, you will reach a sign for Indian Spring at about the 1-mile mark. The spring, said to have been used by Indians years ago as a water source, lies just 10 yards beyond the sign. Although it is hidden by a stone and cement structure built to maintain the water's purity, you may be able to see the water bubbling up from the ground just downstream. Evidence of long-ago Indian inhabitants includes an ancient Indian burial grounds on the refuge property.

Backtrack 20 yards and veer right (north)—looking for white blazes—and head immediately up the slope of an *esker,* a geological feature created when the glacial ice melted. You will notice that the esker supports very little vegetation due to the poor quality of the soil. Travel the top of the esker for about 0.1 mile and turn right (northeast) at a trail junction on the downslope of the esker at 1.25 miles. (Do not follow the trail back to the entrance as indicated by the sign.) Less than 0.1 mile later, as you walk for several hundred yards between the perfect rows of towering pine trees, children will no doubt be tempted to stray off the straight path to wind among the trees. Double blazes indicate a left-hand turn as you march past the final pine soldier. While you travel along the river's edge for about 1 mile, point out to the children the tremendous examples of beaver activity. Challenge your children to find the large oak trees that have been killed by the beavers. (Beavers don't eat the oaks but they have already consumed their favorite trees and need to wear down their teeth. Suggest that they look up to locate the trees that are without leaves and obviously dead, then look down at the tree's base to find the girdle of teeth marks.) In some areas where the river bank is accessible and sandy, children can scamper to the water's edge and look for rainbow and brook trout in the clear water. They may even spot a snapping turtle. About 0.5 mile into the river walk, the trail skirts up a ridge with a sharp, 30-foot dropoff to the water's edge. Beyond this crest, continue to follow the white blazes, avoiding a number of side trails and crossing over tributaries and swampy areas on sturdy bridges.

The trail finally turns away from the water, heads up a moderated grade through pines, and then meanders gradually back toward the entrance through terrain similar to that on the early part of the walk. Deer tracks and droppings, evidence of the large deer population within the refuge, are abundant along the trails. A path marked in yellow and white joins the white-blazed trail at a woods road 2.3 miles from the start; turn right (north) to reach an overlook in 0.3 mile. Here, an elaborate stone bench allows hikers to rest while they take in the expansive view of Little River Valley. (Picnicking is prohibited.) Return to the white-blazed trail that turns right off the woods road and leads back to the entrance and your car in another 0.4 mile.

29. Mashamoquet Brook State Park

Type:	Dayhike or overnight
Difficulty:	Moderate for children
Distance:	4 miles, loop
Hiking time:	3 hours
High point/elevation gain:	520 feet, 290 feet
Hikable:	April–November
Maps:	USGS Danielson

This walk offers two special things for kids to look forward to: the stone Indian Chair perched on a ledge overlook and the famous Putnam Wolf Den, a cave that extends back into the rocky hillside as far as you can see. As the story goes, the state's last wolf was shot here in the winter of 1742. After a wolf killed and injured a number of his sheep, Israel Putnam (later a Revolutionary War hero) set off in search of the wolf's lair. Several days and 35 miles later, he and a group of nearby farmers followed the wolf tracks to the now-famous den. When the first two plans—smoking the wolf out and sending in the dogs—failed, Putnam took matters into his own hands, squeezing through the long, dark tunnel with a torch and musket. After being driven back once by the beast, he shot it on his second attempt and on his third effort, hauled the carcass out of the cave to the cheers of his astounded neighbors. The park offers camping at the Wolf Den and Mashamoquet Brook Campgrounds and swimming at the bypass pool less than one-half mile from the park entrance off of US 44.

Travel to the junction of US 44 and CT-101 in Pomfret. On CT-101, just 200 yards east of the junction, take Wolf Den Drive

The Indian Chair is a comfortable spot for adjusting boots.

0.7 mile. Turn left into the Mashamoquet overflow parking area and leave your car here.

To begin the hike, cross Wolf Den Drive to a well-maintained, blue-blazed trail, walking through a stone wall past a rock marked "Mashamoquet." Double blazes provide clear indications of sudden changes in trail direction. In 0.1 mile, cross a footbridge over a small stream; at 0.2 mile, cross a larger stream. (The name "Mashamoquet" is an Indian word meaning "stream of good fishing.") You will travel alongside and cut through numerous stone walls in the first 0.5 mile. At the 0.5-mile mark, turn right; the trail, a woods road, is now marked with red-and-blue blazes. One-tenth of a mile later, the trail begins a lengthy stretch with a considerable dropoff to the right. The red trail turns left at 0.8 mile; you follow the blue-blazed trail that contin-

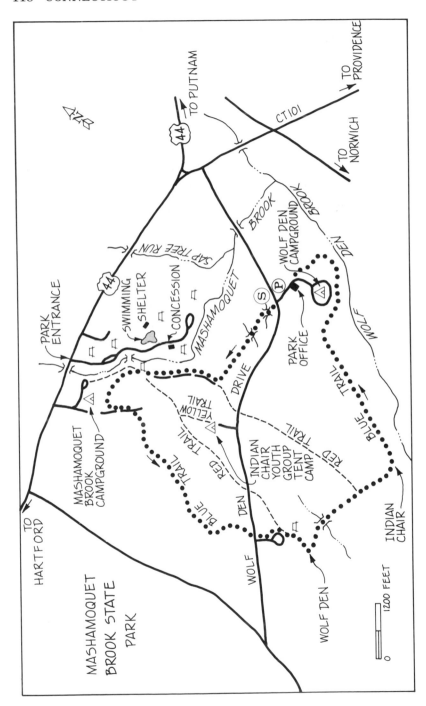

ues straight. This path meanders over streams and up a gradual hill over the next 0.4 mile. At 1.1 miles, double blazes indicate a left turn onto a wooded road; shortly thereafter turn right back onto a wooded path. Climb a gradual hill, then skirt the edge of a field at 1.3 miles.

The trail merges onto Wolf Den Drive at 2 miles; head right across the road (with an eye on little children) to the entrance marked "Wolf Den Trail," carved in stone. Follow the parking area road 0.1 mile, still marked by blue blazes, where a sign carved in a granite boulder indicates that the trail curls back into the woods. These chiseled signs are frequent along this section of trail. (If you prefer a shorter hike, you can park here, 1 mile beyond the first parking lot on Wolf Den Drive. Hike past the Wolf Den to the Indian Chair and back for a total hike of just over 1 mile.) The red trail soon joins the blue; follow a rocky descent for 0.15 mile. Timbers and stone steps make it easily negotiable for younger children. Look for the Wolf Den penetrating the hillside on the right side of the trail. How far inside the very dark and very narrow cave will the kids venture? Be sure to repeat the Wolf Den tale at the cave site so that they will fully appreciate Mr. Putnam's effort.

As the red- and blue-blazed trail continues on a substantial descent, turn around to see more caves dotting the rocky hill. Again, a sturdy footbridge facilitates a wide stream crossing. At 2.6 miles, the red trail splits off to the left; but you remain on the blue trail. Look for more caves and overhangs. The Indian Chair perches on the edge of a steep cliff at the 2.75-mile mark, just off the trail. Kids can climb on the chair (it makes a great photo!) but should be warned to stay well back from cliff's edge. Return to the trail and continue descending before traversing an area of rocky ups and downs. After skirting a field at 3.7 miles, the trail reenters the woods, passing a wet area created by beavers. The trail eventually brings you to a dirt path in the Wolf Den camping area that leads to your car.

MASSACHUSETTS

---

30. Bash Bish Falls

Type: Dayhike
Difficulty: Moderate for children
Distance: 3.7 miles, round trip
Hiking time: 3.5 hours
High point/elevation gain: 1500 feet, 840 feet
Hikable: May–November
Maps: USGS Bash Bish Falls

This is a spectacular waterfall by anyone's standards. At its most dramatic point, a huge boulder splits the river and sends the water plunging into a deep pool in a set of twin falls. Flat, poolside rocks and and worn trails climbing alongside the falls provide several points from which to watch the cascading water. Although the falls may have a number of visitors when you arrive, it's likely you'll be one of the few who hiked 3 miles to get there, because it is also accessible from Bash Bish Road by an emergency vehicle road.

 From the junction of MA-23 and MA-41 in South Egremont, drive 0.25 mile south on MA-41. Turn right onto Mount Washington Road. (At 1.6 miles, a sign says "To Mount Washington State Park"). In 7.4 miles, turn right onto Bash Bish Road where a sign indicates that Bash Bish Falls is 4 miles away. In 1.6 miles, turn left at another sign: "Bash Bish Falls, 2 miles." At 1.3 miles, pass the upper parking lot to the falls. Continue for another mile into New York state (where the road becomes NY-344) to a park entrance on the left.

Cross the Bash Bish Brook on the park road. Instruct the kids to look for the white blazes of the South Taconic Trail bordering the right-hand side of the park road. Soon, the white-blazed trail turns right (south), heading away from the brook. Pass a building with rest facilities and head into the woods on a moderate grade, now traveling alongside a swift tributary of the Bash Bish Brook. At double blazes, the trail turns right and joins a tote road. Soon

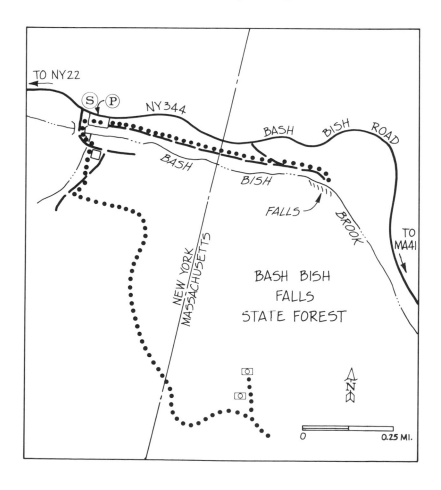

Resting beside Bash Bish Falls

the trail curls left, leaving the stream behind. Double blazes guide you left off the tote road, farther away from the stream on a continuous, moderately steep ascent. The trail momentarily levels out and, far below, you can hear the sound of the rushing Bash Bish Brook. Ask the kids to name the colors they see in the forest—it may seem entirely green until they start examining the flora and fauna a little more closely.

Bending right (south), the path resumes its moderate climb through mixed hardwoods and thickets of mountain laurel. Again, you will have a short reprieve from the climb before the trail winds left (east) and climbs to a small stream that trickles in from the right. After one further ascent, 1 mile from the start, you arrive at an intersection with a blue-blazed side trail leading left (northwest) to views. Follow the side trail to the rock painted with triple blue blazes. From here, enjoy the hike's only views over a bucolic setting and adjoining ridges. Because picnicking is not allowed near the falls, stop here for a snack.

Return to the parking area where you left your car and travel in an easterly direction along a woods road on the north side of Bash Bish Brook, entering Bash Bish Falls State Forest in Massachusetts. (Note that no swimming or picnicking is allowed in the Bash Bish Falls State Forest.) In 0.55 mile, the footpath joins an emergency vehicle road, and in another 0.15 mile, you'll arrive at the falls. "Ooooh" and "aaaah" with the other visitors and relax on the boulders lining the falls before returning to your car.

31. Race Brook Falls and Mount Everett

Type:	Dayhike or overnight
Difficulty:	Difficult for children
Distance:	5 miles, round trip
Hiking time:	5 hours
High point/elevation gain:	2602 feet, 1850 feet
Hikable:	April–October
Maps:	USGS Bash Bish Falls

On the first warm day in April, take your older children on a hike along Race Brook. You'll witness the torrent of icy water crashing down the rocky hillside in this Massachusetts wilderness and then climb to the windswept summit of Mount Everett. But be prepared—this is one of the toughest hikes in the book. It includes a walk along part of the Appalachian Trail, the path that winds over the backbone of the Appalachian Mountain range for 2050 miles from Georgia to Maine. The first section of the trail was blazed in 1922 and the final stretch in 1938; in 1968, Congress proclaimed the Appalachian Trail a National Scenic Trail, to be maintained as a hiking path forever. Thanks to the efforts of volunteers affiliated with the Appalachian Trail Conference, the trail is regularly maintained and reblazed.

From the junction of MA-41 and MA-23 in South Egremont, travel south on MA-41 for 5 miles. At the intersection with Salisbury Road, park on the right-hand (west) side of MA-41 in a paved turnaround.

The trail leads from the middle of the parking loop, heading initially west then immediately southwest along blue triangular blazing. This, the Race Brook Trail, cuts across a swampy area then bends to the right (west), skirting the right-hand side of a field. The path dives into a hemlock grove on a mild ascent. At a trail junction 0.2 mile from the start, veer left, guided by the sign for the "Appalachian Trail via Falls, 2 miles." Still following the blue blazes, you will drop down to the bank of Race Brook at 0.3 mile. On a steamy day, you will notice that the temperature plummets as you enter the ravine.

The trail follows the north bank briefly then crosses to the southern side on stepping stones, turning left up a grade then switching right to resume its westerly course. The path now climbs with conviction, leading away from the brook (the original riverside trail has been rerouted due to erosion). Soon, the river is out of sight, although the sound of running water far below is still evident. At close to 0.5 mile, a red-blazed side trail leads to the middle falls. Walk 200 yards along relatively level ground to this spectacular waterfall; be careful if you elect to climb down to the bottom of the falls—the trail is quite steep. Kids should probably view the falls from the trail.

Return to the blue-blazed trail and turn right as the relentless ascent continues along a spongy path. At 0.8 mile, the trail cuts northeast along flatter terrain, crossing Race Brook at the bottom of the upper falls. Torrents of water crash down the rocky groove some 80 feet, then continue splashing along the banks of

Race Brook. Pause here to let the kids catch their breath and enjoy the falls before attacking the next stiff climb.

The trail leaves the falls, heading north on a moderate, then steep ascent. In 0.2 mile, the path turns southwest on more level ground, running along a rocky ridge. As you approach the far end of this ridge, enjoy the fine views down the valley into Connecticut. The trail rejoins Race Brook on a mild ascent and soon crosses it on a log bridge. Here, the slow-moving brook beckons to hot, sticky hikers. The kids can roll up their pant legs and wade in the cool pools.

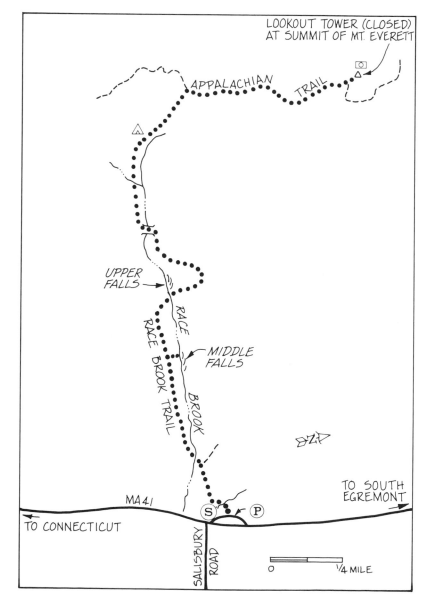

As you continue, you'll crisscross some tributaries to Race Brook, now just a trickling stream. Soon, it will disappear. On the left, on level ground, is a hidden campsite (0.25 mile before the Appalachian Trail junction). Two miles from the start, the Race Brook Trail ends rather anticlimactically at an intersection with the Appalachian Trail. Turn right and begin the steep, rocky as-

Race Brook's middle falls

cent to the summit of Mount Everett. Point out to the kids the stunted trees such as scrub pitch pine and the low groundcovers of blueberry and huckleberry bushes, indications of the high altitude and fierce winds. You'll pass an occasional bald face with superb views south and east as you near the peak. With your first glimpse of the lookout tower that rises from the summit, you'll feel the burst of energy necessary to complete the first half of the hike. Although the tower is closed, the gently sloping summit offers near-360-degree views, taking in Mount Greylock to the north and Bear Mountain to the south.

After a well-deserved and much-needed break, refuel with some high-energy snacks. On the return trip, witness the "birth of a brook" as Race Brook grows from a tiny ribbon of water to a forcefully flowing brook. Return to your car as you came, punctuating the descent with frequent compliments for your young, hardworking hiking companions.

32. Devil's Pulpit and Squaw Peak

Type:	Dayhike
Difficulty:	Moderate for children
Distance:	2.8 miles, loop
Hiking time:	3 hours
High point/elevation gain:	1642 feet, 900 feet
Hikable:	April–November
Maps:	USGS Great Barrington/ Stockbridge

There is no question that this is the real thing—a true mountain. The climb is steady and the effort is well rewarded by breathtaking panoramas from atop the rocky summit called Squaw Peak. According to ancient folklore, an Indian maiden was hurled from the mountaintop because she fell in love with a brave from an enemy tribe. On the mountain's southern slope is a stone cairn that is supposed to have been built by sympathetic Indians as a monument to the maiden. Our three-year-old led the way to the top, but it may be tough going on some little legs. You might

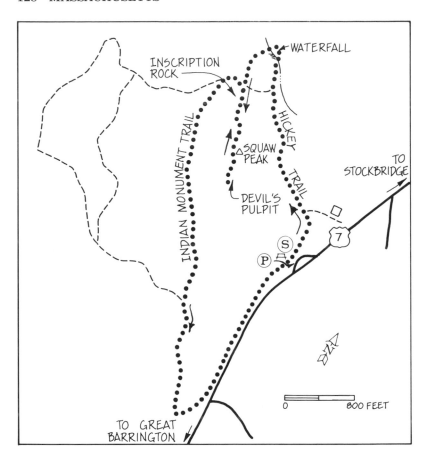

want to do as we did and carry an empty child carrier for the smaller one whose initial intentions were nobler than his or her stamina.

From Stockbridge center, drive south for 3.0 miles on US 7 to a parking and picnic area on the right (you'll see a sign for Monument Mountain Reservation just before this area). If you're coming from Great Barrington, from the junction of MA-23 and US 7, travel north on US 7 for 3.0 miles to the parking area on the left.

The white-blazed Hickey Trail heads north from the parking area near the trail map—a sign indicates that this is the "Steep Trail" (the other choice being the "Easy Trail"). You'll be completing the loop by returning via the Easy Trail, since most hikers agree that it is easier to ascend rather than descend a steep grade. The path heads off through a mixed hardwood forest on

Atop Devil's Pulpit

fairly level ground for the first 0.3 mile. Climbing can be laborious for little tykes; we play memory games to take the kids' minds off of their tiring legs. Start off by trying to name the Ten Essentials (from our introduction) and move on to the names of the Seven Dwarves, TV characters, residents of Sesame Street, and so on. When they are reminding one another about Grumpy and Sneezy, they will be less likely to complain.

Soon, the tempo changes as the trail begins its steep ascent. The path is just rocky enough to provide good footholds. Early on, short side trails lead around muddy areas; at the first true trail intersection at 0.5 mile where white blazes split off in two directions, continue straight following along the stream. You will pass a waterfall on the left 0.1 mile later (the water trickles off of an overhanging boulder) and travel on level ground until a trail joins from the left. Continue straight here and go straight again in another 30 yards when a trail joins from the right. You will soon arrive at Inscription Rock, which tells of the conveyance of land to The Trustees of Reservations and the intention that this property be a "place of free enjoyment for all time."

 Just beyond the rock you will begin a short, rugged climb to Squaw Peak, the highest point in the reservation. Squaw Peak is essentially a 0.3-mile-long ridge that narrows to less than 20 feet wide in some places. At this summit, 1.2 miles from the start, stand atop impressive outcroppings of granite with spectacular views of the eastern valley and the Berkshires. Look for the Housatonic, Williams, and Green rivers winding through the lush valley. Just beyond Squaw Peak is Profile Rock, which, viewed from the south, resembles an Indian's head. Devil's Pulpit, a pinnacle on the summit's eastern side, is frequented by rock climbers. Retrace your steps past Inscription Rock to the trail intersection and turn left, gently beginning your descent. At the next trail intersection, bear left onto Indian Monument Trail and follow this path as it gradually descends the mountain along the base of the cliffs. Always bear left, as unmarked trails split off to the right. (Remember to use the memory game to distract fussy hikers, young or old.) Soon the path becomes a woods road that eventually leaves the forest and joins US 7. Walk for a short distance on the highway to the parking area and your car.

33. Laura's Lookout and Ice Glen

Type: Dayhike
Difficulty: Moderate for children
Distance: 4 miles, loop
Hiking time: 3.5 hours
High point/elevation gain: 1465 feet, 850 feet
Hikable: April–November
Maps: USGS Stockbridge

Ice Glen is magnificent in the spring when the meltwaters freeze and produce natural ice sculptures that cling to the cliffs and boulders. It is also very dangerous then because hikers are forced to scramble over ice-covered rocks and crevices. The glen is also an exciting place to be on Halloween, when Stockbridge folks make their way through this maze of boulders carrying torches. But the best time for a family to visit this dark gorge is on a day in August, since the shape and depth of the ravine ensure that even on the steamiest of summer days, it will be "air-conditioned." Before tackling the glen, stroll through the woods to Laura's Lookout for a lovely view of the area surrounding historic Stockbridge.

From the center of Stockbridge, drive south 0.2 mile on US 7. Turn left on Park Street and drive 0.4 mile to the road's end. Park in the circle.

Study the trail map before starting off on the path marked with blue blazes that exits the east side of the parking circle. Cross the Housatonic River on a suspension footbridge and make your way over unused railroad tracks. After traveling under some power lines, you will head into the woods, climbing gradually. At a fork in the trail at 0.4 mile, bear left and follow the trail as it gradually ascends for about 0.7 mile and arrives at an observation tower at Laura's Lookout. Do the smaller kids get bored with nothing but trees to look at on either side of the trail? Walking through the woods is more fun if you pretend to be a stalking tiger, bouncy bear cub, or wild horse.

After enjoying the pretty views of the surrounding country-side from the lookout, retrace your steps to the junction and turn left on the blue-blazed Ice Glen Trail. Within 0.3 mile, the firm dirt path becomes the boulder-strewn ravine that is the Ice Glen. The blazes lead you on a twisted route through mazes of stone on the floor of the gorge that form interesting caves and tunnels. The moss-covered rocks can be slippery, especially after a rain. Some small children will need assistance through the gorge while others will insist on scaling the boulders alone. If you need to moti-vate little children who are becoming tired climbing through the

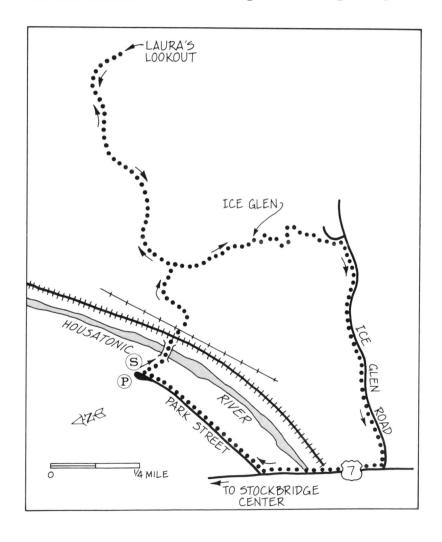

glen, look ahead and point out a good "resting rock." Urge the kids to scramble to that spot for a break and then ask them to select the next resting rock farther ahead.

After a 0.4-mile walk through the ravine, you will emerge on a wooded path and in 0.1 mile arrive at a private driveway. Continue straight down the steep drive to Ice Glen Road. Turn right here and walk 0.7 mile to US 7; turn right and in 0.3 mile, turn right onto Park Street. Along these roads bordering Stockbridge, count green cars or people wearing hats or brown dogs. Walk down Park Street to where your car is parked.

Suspension footbridge over the Housatonic River

Pristine Berry Pond

34. Berry Pond

Type:	Dayhike or overnight
Difficulty:	Moderate for children
Distance:	4.8 miles, loop
Hiking time:	5 hours
High point/elevation gain:	2313 feet, 1300 feet
Hikable:	May–November
Maps:	USGS Pittsfield West

Although you are likely to find strawberries, blueberries, or raspberries along the trail to Berry Pond (depending, of course, on the season), the pond gets its name not from the trailside fruit but from William Berry, one of George Washington's soldiers who owned land in the Berkshires. At just over 2000 feet, Berry Pond is said to be the highest natural body of water in the state. Although swimming is not allowed, kids can look for bullfrogs or fish in the clear water while the adults relax on the grassy bank.

From US 7, turn west onto West Street in the center of Pittsfield. Drive 2.6 miles; turn right onto Churchill Street. In 1.6 miles, turn left onto unmarked Cascade Street (just after a sign for Pittsfield State Forest). Follow this road for another 0.5 mile. At an intersection, turn right and you will see the entrance for Pittsfield State Forest. Proceed through the entrance and bear right on Berry Pond Circuit Road. Drive 0.6 mile to a parking lot on the left.

From the parking area, look across the stream to the remnants of a ski jump that kids may want to explore before or after the hike. Head left out of the parking area, up Berry Pond Circuit Road. In about 0.1 mile, double blue triangular blazes indicate a left turn (west) off of the paved road and onto a jeep road. Shortly, an elevated platform appears on your left: the top of the ski jump. Ever been curious about the view a ski jumper has before launching himself down the chute? Have the children take a look.

Past the ski jump, you reach an intersection and continue straight, on a slight ascent. In another 0.1 mile, turn right (north) at a second intersection, now following a red-blazed jeep road. Although this, the Turner Trail, is not heavily blazed, no side roads or intersections will confuse you. After a straight and steady climb of nearly a mile, you will see the radio tower on top of Berry Mountain through the trees. At an intersection, on fairly level ground, continue straight, still following the painted red blazes. Soon, Berry Pond comes into view and the trail sweeps right, skirting the pond. Side trails provide access to the water's edge. The main trail departs the pond and enters a field, the site of the Berkshire Hills Ramble, a self-guided nature walk. At the paved road, turn left and follow it to Berry Pond. The westward view of New York's Adirondacks and Catskills is spectacular and well worth a lengthy pause. At Berry Pond, enjoy your picnic lunch or set up camp. Follow the pond outlet across Berry Pond Circuit Road to watch the water cascade down this high ridge.

To continue your hike, walk back up the road the way you came for 0.1 mile, watching for the white blazes that mark the Taconic Skyline Trail. Follow the blazes into the woods on the left-hand side of the road and climb to the top of Berry Hill. The trail quickly emerges onto the road; turn left. The white-blazed Taconic Skyline Trail departs the road almost immediately, left, into the woods. Continue your steady descent along paved Berry

Pond Circuit Road for another 0.2 mile, watching for the wide trail head on the left that will take you in a northerly direction over Lulu Brook. At an intersection with the equally wide Lulu

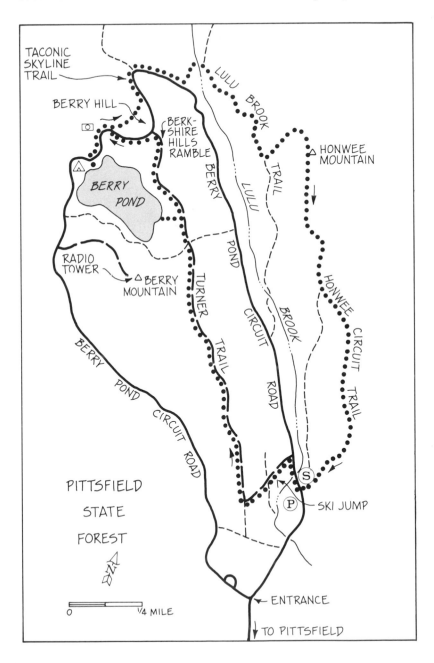

TACONIC
SKYLINE
TRAIL

BERRY HILL

BERK-
SHIRE
HILLS
RAMBLE

BERRY POND

RADIO
TOWER

BERRY
MOUNTAIN

LULU BROOK TRAIL

HONWEE
MOUNTAIN

LULU BROOK

BERRY POND CIRCUIT ROAD

TURNER TRAIL

HONWEE CIRCUIT TRAIL

BERRY POND CIRCUIT ROAD

PITTSFIELD

STATE

FOREST

N

0   ¼ MILE

S

P   SKI JUMP

ENTRANCE

TO PITTSFIELD

Brook Trail, turn right (southeast). In 0.5 mile, head left at a junction with the Honwee Circuit Trail. (Note that any trail leading to the right will return you to Berry Pond Circuit Road and, eventually, your car.) This trail winds northeast over the blueberry-covered Honwee Mountain then heads southeast for a long steady descent, following blue blazes, to the Berry Pond Circuit Road. You will emerge from the woods across the road from the parking lot and your car.

35. March Cataract Falls

Type:	Dayhike or overnight
Difficulty:	Moderate for children
Distance:	4.4 miles, round trip
Hiking time:	4 hours
High point/elevation gain:	3491 feet, 1250 feet
Hikable:	May–October
Maps:	USGS Williamstown

From the War Memorial tower on the summit of the state's highest mountain, kids will be able to see New Hampshire's Mount Monadnock and the Adirondacks (115 miles away). In addition to the auto roads, nearly a dozen trails, including the Appalachian Trail, lead to the peak of Mount Greylock in Mount Greylock State Reservation. Sneakers won't do on this hike—the climbs and descents are challenging, especially as you drop into the ravine toward the waterfall. Smaller children or those with little hiking experience may find this one too demanding.

From US 7 in Lanesborough, turn onto North Main Street, heading east, following a sign to "Mount Greylock Reservation, 10." In 1 mile, at the Mount Greylock Visitor Center, pick up a trail map. Continue on the same road (now called Rockwell Road) for another 9 miles to the summit of Mount Greylock. Park here. (From MA-2, west of North Adams, turn south on Notch Road and drive about 8 miles to the junction with Rockwell Road. Turn left and shortly arrive at the summit parking lot.)

From the parking lot, head to the radio tower. To the left of the radio tower and behind the adjacent building, the blue-blazed

War Memorial tower on the Mount Greylock summit

Overlook Trail begins a modest descent. This wide path acts as a stream bed during the rainy spring season (waterproof footwear is recommended then). In 0.3 mile, the trail crosses Notch Road and reenters the woods on a new section of trail that is somewhat indistinct but well blazed. After a short descent, old and new Overlook Trails merge and the path again is worn and easy to follow. The trail continues modestly downhill as it cuts a path along the rim of Greylock. Any complainers? Play "What do we hear?" It may seem quiet until the kids listen for sounds like the wind blowing, leaves rustling, birds chirping, the drone of an airplane overhead. At 0.7 mile, the first of two side paths leads right to an overlook (thus the trail name). After each side trip, return to the main path.

At 1 mile, the trail descends to a stream crossing then ascends briefly but steeply and arrives at the intersection with the blue-blazed Hopper Trail. Turn right and drop moderately down

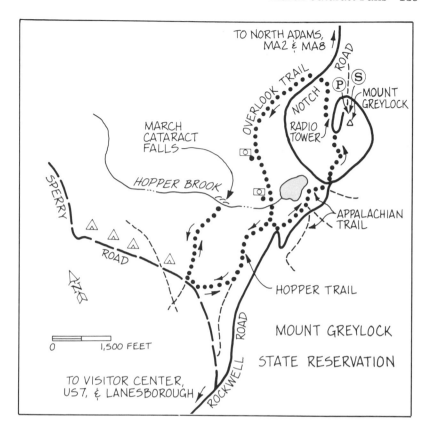

to an intersection with Deer Hill Trail. Bear right, continuing on the Hopper Trail to an intersection with Sperry Road near the Sperry Campground at 1.6 miles. Turn right and walk along the road into the campground; shortly signs and a trail for March Cataract Falls appear on your right. The sign indicates that a mile-long, rugged trail will bring you to the falls. Actually, it is closer to a 0.6-mile journey. Although this section of trail will be tough for little guys, especially as you get closer to the falls, the trip is worth the effort. The icy cold water tumbles down the side of Greylock, generously spraying anyone who needs cooling off. Take pictures of the kids cautiously approaching the misty water-fall. The idea of getting drenched may be appealing to them now, but just wait until they start climbing back up the hillside with heavy, water-soaked pants. (A handful of chocolate-covered raisins for the one who complains the least!)

To begin the return hike, reverse your direction and climb back up the mountainside on the Hopper Trail. At the intersection with the Overlook Trail, bear right, still on the Hopper Trail. The trail soon outlets on Rockwell Road, then immediately turns left and reenters the woods. Rejoin Rockwell Road at the end of Hopper Trail. Here, join the white-blazed Appalachian Trail. Follow the signs to the summit. You will cross Notch Road at the intersection with Rockwell Road and head northeast back into the woods. In 0.3 mile, you will arrive at your car. Before you leave, visit the tower to take in the best views Massachusetts has to offer.

36. Money Brook Trail

Type: Dayhike or overnight
Difficulty: Difficult for children
Distance: 4 miles, loop
Hiking time: 5 hours
High point/elevation gain: 2690 feet, 1400 feet
Hikable: May–October
Maps: USGS Williamstown

Mount Greylock is not a place to bring the family on a first or second outing. Though the trails are well worn and the blazes freshly painted, most of the paths snaking along the side of this mountain are too steep and rugged for inexperienced hikers, young children, or anyone without proper hiking gear. The reward for finishing this loop is a rest near the awesome Money Brook Falls and the realization that you have completed one of the state's most difficult 4-mile hikes.

 Just west of North Adams center on MA-2, head south on Notch Road. Drive 5.0 miles to a two-car parking area and well-marked trail head on the right-hand side of the road. From the summit of Greylock (the junction of Rockwell and Notch roads), travel 3.1 miles on Notch Road to the small parking area on the left. The sign here says "Short Cut to Money Brook Trail and Money Brook Falls."

Follow the trail indicated by blue triangular blazes down a moderate descent to a junction with the Money Brook Trail, marked with blue rectangular blazes. (Having second thoughts because your 10-year-old's new boots pinch her toes? Turn left

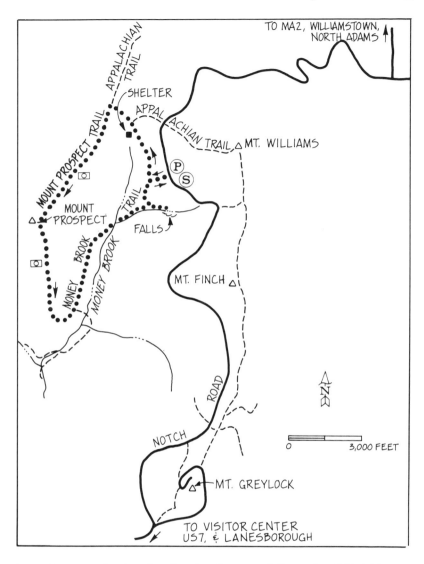

here for a total trip of under 1 mile to and from the falls.) To continue the long loop, turn right on Money Brook, passing a shelter for campers at 0.55 mile, and at 0.6 mile join the white-blazed Appalachian Trail. Continue straight, now on the Appalachian Trail, and shortly make a left-hand (south) turn onto the blue-blazed Mount Prospect Trail as the Appalachian Trail heads right. The trail ascends moderately and provides excellent views of the mountains and valleys to the west.

After 0.8 mile of easy climbing, you will reach the summit of

Mount Prospect. (Tell the kids they've gone almost halfway!) The trail then drops steeply, providing superb views of Mount Greylock and reaches a junction with Money Brook Trail, 0.8 mile from the Prospect summit. Arrows painted on a rock at this intersection indicate that the Money Brook Trail goes left or right. You turn left and climb high above the rushing Money Brook for 0.5 mile on a trail that cuts precariously into the steep ridge of Mount Prospect. You will eventually cross a tributary of Money Brook and hike up a very steep, short ascent. Did the kids make it up that hill without a complaint? Give them a pat on the back! The trail reaches an intersection on a switchback. Travel straight for a short (0.1-mile) side trip following the sign to Money Brook Falls, a spectacular waterfall that drops some 50 feet before tum-

A careful descent beside Money Brook Falls

bling down a series of cascades. After relaxing by the falls, return to the junction at the sign for the falls and bear right on an ascent. Soon you will arrive at the intersection with the trail marked by blue triangular blazes. Turn right here and wearily travel the final ascent to your car. Congratulations!

37. Pine Cobble Trail

Type: Dayhike
Difficulty: Moderate for children
Distance: 3.2 miles, round trip
Hiking time: 3 hours
High point/elevation gain: 1894 feet, 1000 feet
Hikable: April–November
Maps: USGS Williamstown

This trail, a favorite among Williams College students, begins just a short distance from campus. It is a family favorite as well because the well-worn path means that even children not yet adept at following blazes can lead the hike. The ascent is continuous and rocky at times, but with a few rest stops children should have no trouble reaching the large, open summit. There, they will delight in scaling the quartzite boulders while the adults take in the expansive view of the valley and nearby mountain ranges.

Take MA-2 (Main Street) in Williamstown to Cole Avenue. Turn north on Cole Avenue and cross the Hoosic River and railroad tracks, arriving at a T intersection. Cross the intersection bearing right and head up a narrow, private road with houses on each side. Less than 0.1 mile up the road, look for a sign on the left indicating the start of the Pine Cobble Trail. (Construction in the area has caused the first section of trail to be rerouted.)

Marked with triangular blue blazes, the trail ascends steadily with few level areas and some steep climbs. At 0.8 mile, just beyond a relatively flat section, the trail bears left and a side trail on the right leads to Bear Spring. At the 1-mile mark, a sign points back down the trail toward Williamstown. Ascending again, cross a boulder field and then a seasonal brook before heading up a carved-out section of trail that acts as a stream bed in the spring. Kids may want to collect some of the pinkish rocks

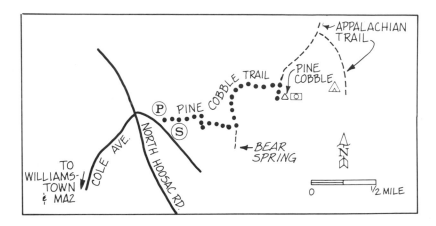

strewn along the path, small samples of the magnificent quartzite outcrop at the peak.

Soon, the trees become shorter and less dense. At the top of the ridge, you are just 0.1 mile from the Pine Cobble summit. An orange-blazed trail leads right to the overlooks while the blue blazes continue left 0.6 mile to the Appalachian Trail. The open, boulder-strewn summit offers a panoramic view of the Williamstown valley. Look toward the south for the tower on the Greylock summit. Due west is the Taconic Range and the Hoosic Range is to the east. Let the kids scramble around on the boulders before enjoying your picnic lunch and returning to your car.

38. Tannery Falls and Balanced Rock

Type:	Dayhike
Difficulty:	Moderate for children
Distance:	3 miles, round trip
Hiking time:	2 hours
High point/elevation gain:	1865 feet, 500 feet
Hikable:	May–November
Maps:	USGS North Adams/Windsor

This hiking route in Savoy Mountain State Forest offers a wooded walk along the river bank to Balanced Rock followed by a short trip to a thundering waterfall that plunges 60 feet into a gorge. The rushing falls are breathtaking, especially in late spring when the river is swollen. Kids and water are a natural combination, and water that seems to be racing to some unknown destination is all that more interesting. Does a stick swim faster than your child can run? Do acorns float? Whose leaf makes a better boat? (If you're interested in staying overnight in the area, Savoy Mountain State Forest offers 45 campsites.)

From the western junction of MA-8A and MA-2 in Charlemont, drive 6.2 miles west on Route 2 to Black Brook Road on the left (just before the "Entering Florida" [Massachusetts] sign on MA-2). Head south on Black Brook Road and drive 1.4 miles to an intersection. Turn right and travel 1 mile; turn right onto Tannery Road and drive 0.8 mile (past a sign for Savoy Mountain State Forest) to the Tannery Falls Parking Area. (Tannery Road is not plowed and during the winter and early spring is impassable.)

Leave the western entrance of the parking area, cross Tannery Road, and join an unmarked (one faded yellow blaze) woods road. In 100 yards, yellow and blue blazes appear on the right and the trail heads for the river's edge. Although the triangular yellow blazes (and occasional blue ones) that you will be following are faded and infrequent, the trail essentially follows along the left bank of Ross Brook. At about the 0.2-mile mark, the river forks; cross the smaller branch to follow the larger, right-hand

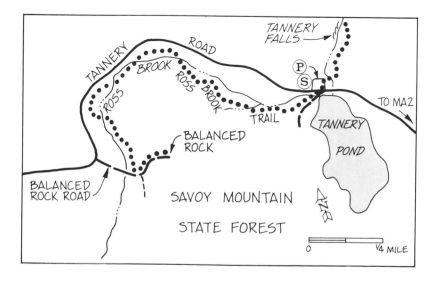

Rugged Tannery Falls

branch. At 0.6 mile, begin a series of brook crossings on random stones that might be difficult for children in the spring or after a heavy rain. The sounds and sights of the splashing river are fun for kids—you might have to make frequent stops while one child chases a frog and another pokes at a miniature, mossy island.

After following along the river for 1.1 miles, turn left onto a dirt road, walk uphill for a short distance, and at 1.25 miles you will reach Balanced Rock, a huge glacial boulder weighing 250 tons that seems to be "balanced" on a bluff. After the kids gingerly examine this unusual boulder, follow the Ross Brook Trail back through the woods to the parking area (or take Balanced Rock Road to Tannery Road and turn right; walk 1 mile to the parking lot.)

From the right-hand corner of the parking area, follow the blue blazes for a short trip to Tannery Falls. This trail parallels the gorge through which the river flows. Although cables are strung along the side of the trail where there are sudden, steep dropoffs, parents should still keep children in constant view here. Exercise extreme caution at the top of the falls. At the overlook, the adults can determine whether or not their young companions should attempt the steep trail to the bottom, where the view is the most impressive. Return to your car via the blue-blazed trail.

39. Granville State Forest

Type:	Dayhike or overnight
Difficulty:	Moderate for children
Distance:	4 miles, loop
Hiking time:	3.5 hours
High point/elevation gain:	1275 feet, 550 feet
Hikable:	July–October
Maps:	USGS West Granville

Who wants to play Huck Finn? Complete with a rock slide down a small waterfall and giant boulders to dive from, the swimming hole near the start of this hike is probably a lot like the ones Grandma and Grandpa used to splash in when they were little tykes. The only concessions to modern times are the lifeguard and bath house nearby. The swimming hole is actually part of Hubbard Brook, the cascading river that accompanies hikers for much of this route through Granville State Forest. Many areas along the riverbank have been adapted for use by campers with fireplaces, picnic tables and other facilities.

From the junction of MA-8 and MA-57 in New Boston, travel east on MA-57 for 6.5 miles and turn right onto West Hartland Road. Drive 1 mile. Just beyond the camping area and bridge over

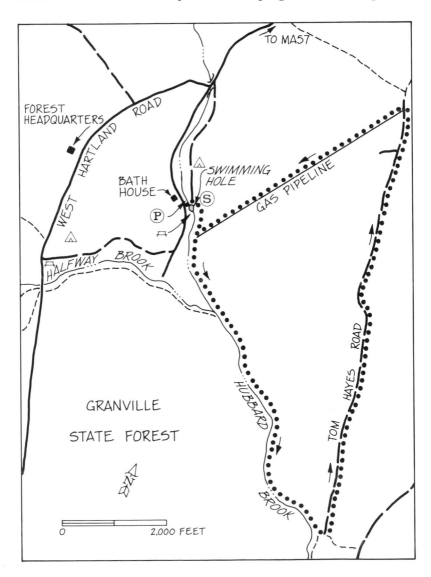

Hubbard Brook's old-time swimming hole

Hubbard Brook, turn left onto a road to the picnic and swimming area. You will arrive at a small parking area on the left in 0.5 mile. (From the western junction of MA-57 and US 202 in Southwick, travel west on MA-57 for 12.1 miles and turn left onto West Hartland Road. Follow the above directions.)

Leave the parking lot and walk through the picnic area. Cross the brook above the falls and swimming hole, selecting stepping stones with caution. An unmarked side trail takes you uphill and slightly left away from the water and in 100 yards intersects a path marked with triangular blue blazes. Turn right onto the path, which soon drops close to the bank of Hubbard Brook. The wide, rocky path descends gradually for the next mile, with the cascading brook racing alongside. The still pools that frequently interrupt the cascades may be impossible for the kids to resist on a muggy summer day.

Near trail's end, after passing through a deep gorge rimmed with hemlocks, the path enters a campfire site at the 1.2-mile mark and exits on the high side of this area onto unmarked Tom Hayes Road, an overgrown jeep path. Turn sharply left onto this rocky road and ascend moderately through unspoiled woods for approximately 1 mile. All that remains of long-ago inhabitants of the land surrounding Hubbard Brook, including Samuel Hubbard who settled here in 1749, are cellar holes and stone walls. In places, the trail has been rerouted to the right of the road due to the deep gullies created by erosion. Near the end of the climb, the trail crosses sets of stone walls. The Tom Hayes Road becomes a usable jeep road at the height of the hill. Within the next 0.3 mile, another jeep road veers left, but you should continue straight. After a short drop followed by an immediate ascent, a cleared swath 75 feet wide bisects the road. On the left, notice the two white relief pipes for an underground gas line. Turn left and follow the rather indistinct trail through this cleared area, heading southwest. Sections of this route may be wet even in late summer.

Continue for nearly 1 mile to the path running parallel to Hubbard Brook. Turn right, paralleling the river. Shortly, the trail will veer right, away from the brook and up a small rise. Atop this hill, look for an unmarked trail heading left (listen for the sound of the waterfall) and in 200 feet you will return to the swimming hole. (If you miss this final left-hand turn, you will arrive at the lower end of the camping area in 0.2 mile.) Dive in!

40. Goat Peak Lookout

Type:	Dayhike
Difficulty:	Easy for children
Distance:	2 miles, round trip
Hiking time:	2 hours
High point/elevation gain:	822 feet, 300 feet
Hikable:	April–November
Maps:	USGS Mount Tom

Mount Tom State Reservation offers 20 miles of well-maintained and well-blazed trails. Although the park may be overcrowded during certain times of the year, several trails (such

The view from Goat Peak

as that to Goat Peak) see less use and are therefore more appealing for those who prefer trees to people while hiking. This trail offers just enough of a challenge to be interesting to the older kids while remaining negotiable for the younger ones. At the summit, you will be rejuvenated by the panoramic views of the Connecticut Valley from the watch tower, one of only two on the reservation. (The annual count of the hawk migration is made from this tower.)

Take Exit 18 off of I-91 in Northhampton (a sign indicates Mount Tom). From the Holyoke-Easthampton town line, drive south on US 5 for 2.1 miles to a sign for the Mount Tom Reservation. Turn right into the reservation; at a T intersection approximately 1.8 miles from US 5, turn left. Travel for 0.1 mile to a side road on the left leading to a parking area next to a maintenance building.

Walk around the gate at the far end of the parking area and soon you will reach the junction of the Metacomet and Monadnock trails. As the crowds head right up the M&M Trail to the Mount Tom summit, you head left (north) on the white-blazed M&M Trail. The trail proceeds through a hemlock forest and, at 0.3 mile, takes a right turn onto a paved road. As you travel the road for several hundred feet, you will pass signs for the Robert Cole Museum of Natural History. This nature museum, housing geology, bird, insect, and small-animal exhibits, is open during the summer months and would make a great post-hike treat for the kids.

After a left-hand turn back into the woods, the path traverses a ridge and passes through another hemlock grove with a foliage ceiling 30 feet above you. Winding gradually uphill through the woods, the path breaks out of the hemlock forest into an area of maples. At the 0.7-mile mark, double blazes signify a right-hand turn to a much steeper section with strategically placed rocks serving as steps (though a little scrambling may be necessary). The trail turns left and continues to climb steeply along a ridge with a rapid drop-off of at least 70 feet just to the left of the path.

As distant views become visible ahead, you'll realize that you are approaching the summit. Double blazes within 150 yards of the top are misleading because the trail obviously continues straight and side trails veer off to the left and right. From the

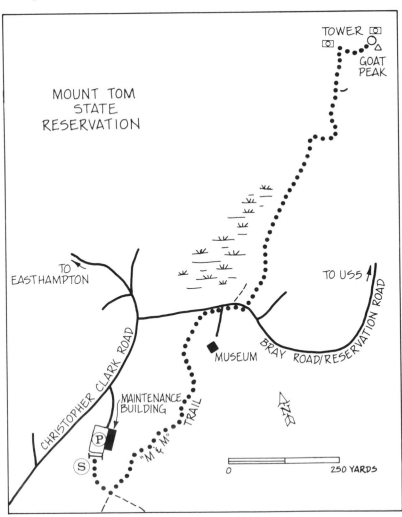

summit spur at 0.9 mile (a good spot for a picnic), the tower is visible to your right, just 200 yards away. While the rocks on the spur afford excellent views of the hustle and bustle of the valley some 700 feet below, a climb up the tower rewards you with a breathtaking panorama in all directions including downtown Springfield to the south, Mount Monadnock to the north, the Berkshires to the west, and Connecticut Valley to the east. The lovely views of Mount Tom prevail as you hike the return trip to your car.

41. Mount Norwottuck and the Horse Caves

Type: Dayhike
Difficulty: Moderate for children
Distance: 3.4 miles, round trip
Hiking time: 3.5 hours
High point/elevation gain: 1106 feet, 600 feet
Hikable: April–November
Maps: USGS Mt. Holyoke

A fairly strenuous climb over well-traveled terrain will take you to the Holyoke Range's highest point atop Mount Norwottuck where the view from the observation tower extends for 70 miles in all directions. The Mount Holyoke summit, accessible by car, is the most popular of the Seven Sisters Hills, but you will enjoy similar views from Norwottuck without having to elbow your way through the crowd. Older kids will relish the challenge of the ascent and enjoy squeezing between the slabs of rock to pass under the Horse Caves, tremendous overhanging ledges beyond the summit. These ledges are said to have sheltered the horses of Daniel Shays and his men during the famous Shays' Rebellion. The second half of the hike, a peaceful woods walk, covers a little more than a mile of fairly level ground along the base of the range.

From the junction of MA-9 and MA-116 in Amherst center,

Horse Caves near the Mount Norwottuck summit

travel south on MA-116 for 4.9 miles to the Notch Visitor Center on the left. Park in the lot adjacent to the building.

The white blazes of the Metacomet and Monadnock Trail will lead you to the summit of Mount Norwottuck and the Horse Caves, while the orange-blazed Robert Frost Trail will guide you back to the visitor center. Initially, you will also be following the Laurel Loop, marked with green leaves inside blue triangles, which begins to the right of the visitor's center. Follow the multi-blazed trail until you reach a dirt road where double blazes indicate a left-hand turn. Immediately following this left turn, take a sharp right (the Laurel Loop continues straight) following white-and-orange blazes. Follow the gravel road under and away from high-tension wires. You may hear the distant crackle of guns from a nearby shooting range. At a set of double white blazes at 0.5 mile, turn right onto the M&M Trail and begin the ascent. Nearly 200 years ago, bears, wolves, and bobcats stalked these woods. Can the kids find traces of today's more common woodland creatures?

Continue straight when a trail appears on the right. The trail climbs steeply to the ridge then rises gently and drops before the final scramble to the summit of Mount Norwottuck at 1.3 miles. From the tower, look north/northeast for Mount Monadnock, west for Mount Greylock, and north/northwest for Mount Ascutney. In the spring or fall, the children can watch for migrating hawks,

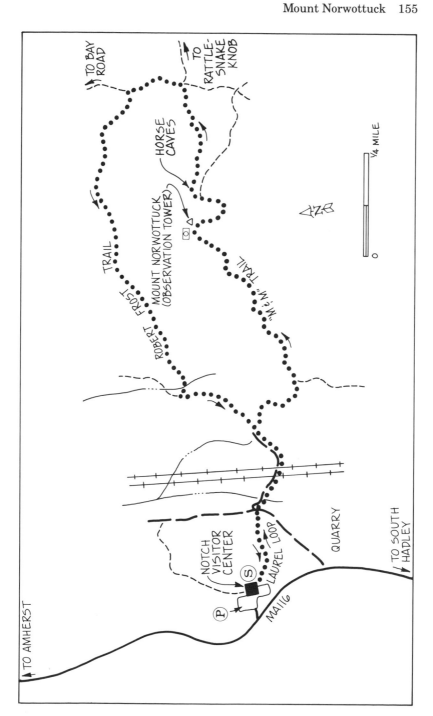

TO AMHERST

TO BAY ROAD

TO RATTLE-SNAKE KNOB

HORSE CAVES

ROBERT FROST TRAIL

MOUNT NORWOTTUCK (OBSERVATION TOWER)

"M.&M." TRAIL

NOTCH VISITOR CENTER

LAUREL LOOP

QUARRY

MA116

TO SOUTH HADLEY

P

S

¼ MILE

0

soaring in "kettles" over the valley. From the summit, head southeast, descending steeply down a rugged path. Just 0.2 mile from the summit, the trail squeezes between a crevice to drop under the Horse Caves. Children may need one parent above and one below to maneuver the tight descent.

Three-tenths of a mile beyond the caves, the trail continues straight to Rattlesnake Knob; you turn left and pick up the orange-blazed Robert Frost Trail. At a crossing with a blue-blazed trail and a sign to Bay Road, turn left, continuing to follow the orange blazes. Point out to the kids that this is a young forest—the original settlers cleared the land for farming and firewood. Logging of the area continued until the mid-1800s. The devastating hurricane of 1938, which left a wide swath of toppled trees and flattened buildings in its wake, also left its mark on this forest. Kids may be able to find evidence of this infamous storm in the rotting trunks that litter the forest floor. After a stream crossing, bear left because the trail has been rerouted to avoid a wet area. With nearly 3 miles completed, the Robert Frost Trail rejoins the white-blazed M&M Trail. Retrace your earlier route to the parking lot.

42. Northfield Mountain

Type: Dayhike
Difficulty: Moderate for children
Distance: 5 miles, round trip
Hiking time: 4 hours
High point/elevation gain: 1100 feet, 900 feet
Hikable: May–November
Maps: USGS Millers Falls

Buried within Northfield Mountain is a pumped-storage generating plant that brings water from the neighboring Connecticut River to a 300-acre reservoir on top of the mountain. At periods of high electrical demand, the water is released and sent through the plant to produce electricity. Northeast Utilities created a recreation facility here for public use with more than 25 miles of well-maintained trails. For a family in relatively good physical condition, this pleasant woods walk to Upper Reservoir's overlook is an excellent first hike. There's little chance of getting lost on the moderate but continuous ascent because the route follows a carriage-width trail with clearly marked and numbered junctions. Frequent trailside maps indicate "You are here." On the return trip, an easy-to-follow wooded path leads past impressive ledges and eventually rejoins the wide path taken on the ascent. Northfield Mountain operates two nearby campgrounds: Barton Cove, situated on a peninsula jutting into the Connecticut River, and Munn's Ferry, located on the river's east bank and accessible only by boat.

From the junction of MA-2 and MA-63 in Turners Falls, take MA-63 north about 2 miles to the Northfield Mountain Recreation Area Visitor Center in Northfield. The center is clearly visible on the right-hand side of the road. Park in the lot near the main building.

At the visitor center, pick up a trail map and a brochure detailing the center's family-oriented recreation and environmental programs.

Northfield Mountain's Rose Ledges

From the large, painted trail map at the rear of the building, look for signs to Jug End Trail and follow it across a field near MA-63 and into the woods. Follow the smooth, narrow gravel road (groomed in the winter for cross-country skiing), watching for sign posts with plaques describing animal tracks and wild-flowers and providing nature facts interesting to children. Kids will also enjoy playing at the various activity stations along the early section of the trail: a balance beam, vault bar, ring ladder, and more.

At a sign for Cedar Circuit, turn left, continuing on Jug End (this intersection is not indicated on the visitor center's trail map). At intersection 6A with 10th Mountain Trail, about 0.5 mile into the hike, Jug End heads diagonally left across the road, crosses a clearing for power lines, and dives back into the woods. Make note of the entrance for the Rose Ledges Trail on the right; you will return by this route. Follow Jug End Trail to intersection 10 with Rock Oak Ramble at 1 mile; head right. Travel 0.4 mile to intersection 16 with Hill 'n Dale and turn left. As the kids weary of the constant uphill grade, distract them with a search for "faces" in tree trunks. After an additional 0.3 mile, Sidewinder Trail heads left (at intersection 22); bear right, still on Hill 'n Dale. Notice the Mariah Foot Trail (intersection 29), heading right into the woods; on the return trip, you will turn off the road here. Just over 2 miles from the start, merge left at intersection 31 with 10th Mountain Trail and follow the level path. (Note the well-supplied first aid kit at the trail intersection.) At intersection 32 go right, up a hill onto a paved road and rotary. Follow the rotary to the right, watching for the trail leading to the reservoir overlook. A large map at the overlook (2.4 miles from the start) explains which mountains are in view. A picnic table offers a pleasant lunch spot.

To return to the visitor center, retrace your steps and turn left at junction 29 (at 3 miles) onto the Mariah Foot Trail following orange plastic blazes. Though the blazes are sparse at times, the trail is well worn and obvious. One-quarter mile beyond the junction, after a gradual ascent, curl right and begin to drop. Keep an eye on the kids on this section of trail because the ground falls off sharply on the left. At junction 33, head left at Deception Pass onto Bumpascutnee Trail through a break in the ledges. As you travel along the base of the cliffs, kids will have a great time investigating the deep channels carved into the ledge's stone face. Who will be the first to see the portion of the cliff that has crumbled? The trail outlets at Yellowjacket Pass at junction 21, nearly

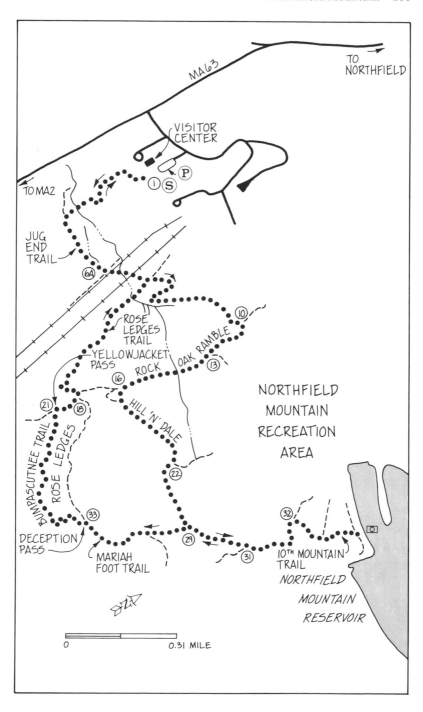

TO
NORTHFIELD

MA63

VISITOR
CENTER

ⓘ Ⓢ Ⓟ

TO MA2

JUG
END
TRAIL

6A

ROSE
LEDGES
TRAIL

YELLOWJACKET
PASS

ROCK

OAK RAMBLE

10

13

16

HILL 'N' DALE

NORTHFIELD
MOUNTAIN
RECREATION
AREA

21

18

BUMPASCUTNEE TRAIL

ROSE LEDGES

22

33

32

DECEPTION
PASS

MARIAH
FOOT TRAIL

29

31

10ᵀᴴ MOUNTAIN
TRAIL

NORTHFIELD
MOUNTAIN
RESERVOIR

N

0   0.31 MILE

4 miles into the hike. Turn right on the gravel road, head up a steep slope and reenter the woods on your left at an orange diamond-blazed trail, the Rose Ledges Trail. High cliffs fall from the left side of the trail and a sign warns hikers of the potential danger. Stay close to your children along this section. The Rose Ledges Trail outlets onto the Jug End Trail at 4.4 miles. Turn left on this trail, following the earlier route back to your car.

43. Quabbin Hill

Type: Dayhike
Difficulty: Moderate for children
Distance: 4.8 miles, loop
Hiking time: 3 hours
High point/elevation gain: 1026 feet, 550 feet
Hikable: April–November
Maps: USGS Windsor Dam

The story of Quabbin Reservoir is fascinating to history buffs and naturalists alike. In the 1920s and 1930s, Quabbin was built as a water supply for metropolitan Boston, and its construction involved the "drowning" of four towns: Enfield, Dana, Prescott, and Greenwich. Today, the 8500 acres called Quabbin Park offer visitors an excellent opportunity for wildlife observation (you may even spot a bald eagle). Unlike most hiking routes, this one begins atop a summit and descends to the water's edge, finishing its loop on a steep ascent to the parking area near the summit tower. Gently rolling terrain combined with fun near the water make this a great hike for kids of most ability levels.

Quabbin Reservoir and the reservation are just off MA-9, west of Worcester and east of Amherst, in Belchertown. Off MA-9, enter the area at a sign for Quabbin Reservation and stop at the visitor center for a map.

Follow the signs to the summit tower, bearing left over Windsor Dam, and park in the lookout tower's parking lot.

Walk to the tower at the opposite end of the parking area for a lovely view of the surrounding mountains and reservoir before

Visiting the Quabbin tower before the hike

locating the trail head at the east side of the parking lot. At the trail head, follow yellow blazes on a gradual descent with distant seasonal views of the reservoir to the right. (Remind the kids to conserve their energy—it will be an uphill finish.) After hiking for 1 mile, cross an open field diagonally left on a grassy road. Follow the road marked with occasional yellow blazes. At an intersection, head right on a dirt road and shortly arrive at a paved road. Children should be accompanied across this road or warned to "look both ways." (A right turn onto the paved road will soon bring you to Enfield Lookout, a favorite spot for bird-watchers with scenic views across the reservoir.)

To head directly for the water's edge, cut straight across the paved road onto the continuation of the wide jeep path. After passing below Enfield Lookout, the trail swings into the woods. A long, gradual descent brings you to the edge of Quabbin Reservoir, nearly 2 miles from the start. Here, paths travel left and right. Ultimately you will head down the right-hand path to complete the loop, but a short walk to the left through the pine plantation provides some good territory for exploration.

As you continue the loop, heading southeast, children will surely prefer to walk the rocky route along water's edge rather than staying on the trail that travels above the reservoir. (Several stream crossings virtually guarantee wet feet in either case.) The kids can get in some stone skipping practice as they stroll along the rocky beach. How far can they get stepping from rock to rock before they slip onto the sand? Soon, the rugged shore gives way to ledge and you must retreat to the trail. After picking your way across a wide, shallow brook that feeds the reservoir, you will enter an open field divided by a grassy road. Head right up the road. (This field would make a great picnic spot; tables are set closer to the paved road. Open fires and camping are prohibited.) Soon you will reach the paved road (0.3 mile from the water). Again, your services as crossing guard are required. Proceed straight across, heading into the woods on a gravel road. The cellar holes bordered by a stone wall on the left serve as a reminder of the lost towns. Follow this road to an intersection with a jeep trail entering from the left. Continue straight for a short distance to a trailhead on your right, 0.55 mile from the paved road. Follow this path on a winding ascent to the top of Quabbin Hill and your car.

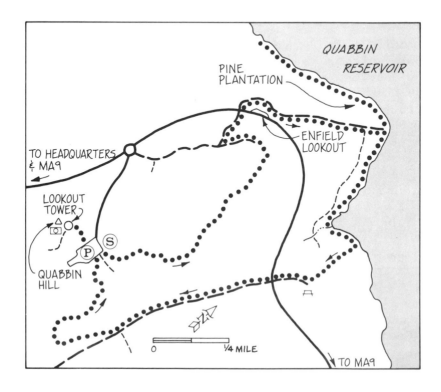

44. Soapstone Hill

Type: Dayhike
Difficulty: Easy for children
Distance: 4 miles, loop
Hiking time: 2.5 hours
High point/elevation gain: 700 feet, 300 feet
Hikable: May–November
Maps: USGS Quabbin Reservoir

Covering 39 square miles with 181 miles of wild shoreline (including island shorelines), Quabbin Reservoir is impressive to look at even on a map and is an oft-cited example of the successful combination of human engineering and natural features. The Metropolitan District Commission manages this property, and does a superb job of maintaining the trails. (No camping is allowed on this MDC property.) Unlike the preceding Quabbin hike, this trail begins in the middle of the woods, seemingly far from the hundreds of thousands of people who visit the area each year. Tell the kids to watch for eagles and red-tailed hawks in the spring, and indications of beaver activity year-round.

From the intersection of MA-122 and US 202 in Orange, travel east on MA-122 for 3.3 miles. Turn right at a sign for the state forest. In just over 1.5 miles, at the end of the paved road and just before an intersection, park off the road on the right.

At the intersection, head right down an unblazed gravel road, quickly climbing a hill and passing under high-tension lines. The road soon levels off at about 0.4 mile and enters a picnic area. A side trail directly across the road heading south will take you to a gorge in another 0.4 mile. Let the kids play on the boulders and explore the ravine's rocky overhangs and small caves. (Watch out for poison ivy!) Retrace your steps and turn left back on the road, heading west toward the reservoir. You will continue to walk past the picnic area. The initially level trail soon begins a modest descent and reaches an intersection at a beaver pond nearly 2 miles from the start. Turn left onto a wide gravel road that leads to an old paved road that once led to the town of Dana. Turn right into the woods heading in a westerly direction (for 20 feet or so) to the water and follow the sandy and rocky shoreline to the right.

Mother Nature supplies a cozy resting spot.

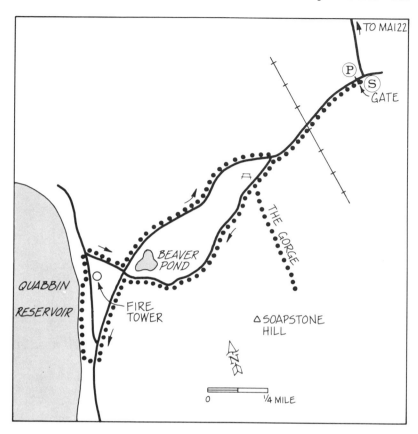

At water's edge, skip stones or collect them (no swimming or wading allowed). Point out to children the tree swallows swooping down over the water. Notice the tree trunks washed ashore, remnants of the clear-cut when the reservoir was first made. As you walk along the shore, you'll see an abandoned fire tower on the right at 2.7 miles. Cut through the brush and join the road that parallels the shoreline. Soon you'll notice another road on the right. Follow this road 0.1 mile back to the intersection at the beaver pond. Here turn left and follow the road up a steady climb. It levels off before merging with the dirt road on which you began your hike, just beyond the picnic area. Continue another 0.35 mile to the paved road, the parking area, and your car.

45. Wachusett Meadow Wildlife Sanctuary

Type: Dayhike
Difficulty: Easy for children
Distance: 2.2 miles, loop
Hiking time: 2 hours
High point/elevation gain: 1050 feet, 170 feet
Hikable: June–November
Maps: USGS Wachusett Mountain

Although the pleasant walk through the fields and woodlands of Wachusett Meadow will delight all members of the family, the 0.5-mile boardwalk near the start of the hike will surely be the kids' favorite part of this trip. Hiking the Swamp Nature Trail may be the only way you will ever be able to explore a wetlands area thoroughly without getting your feet wet. On this 980-acre Audubon property, you are likely to see many open-meadow bird species (such as bobolink and eastern meadowlark) whose populations have declined in other parts of New England as former pasture land has become overgrown.

 From the junction of MA-31 and MA-62 in Princeton center, travel west on MA-62 for 0.6 mile. An Audubon sign indicates a right-hand turn onto Goodnow Road (the road sign may be difficult to read). Drive 1 mile to the sanctuary and turn left into the parking area.

From the parking area, follow the sign to the information center to register, pay your admission fee, and borrow a trail map. (Rest rooms are located in the building to the right of the visitor board.) The hike begins at junction number 1. Head south on the Swamp Nature ("N") Trail, which bisects the large field behind the parking area and sanctuary buildings. At the lower end of the field, the trail enters a red maple swamp on a boardwalk. Follow along the well-maintained boardwalk for 0.5 mile—be sure to let the kids lead the way. Allow them frequent stops to examine the marsh's plant and animal life at the edge of the boardwalk. As you step off this wooden walkway, you'll join the well-worn, blue-blazed trail that winds through the forest. (Blue-blazed trails lead away from the parking area, yellow trails return to the parking

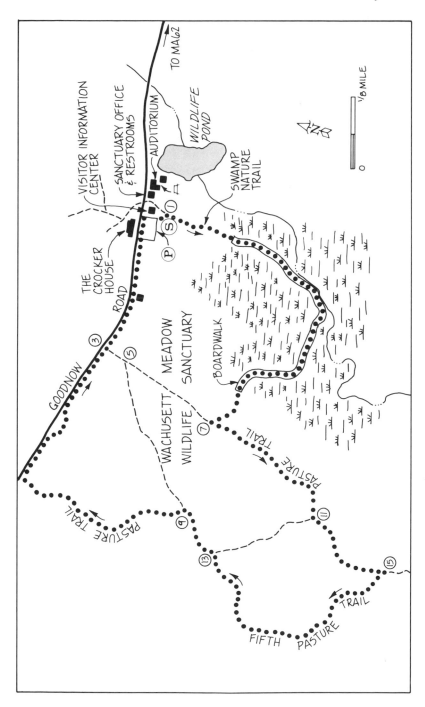

lot and white indicates trails that are considered connecting trails.)

After skirting a field, turn left onto the Pasture ("P") Trail at intersection 7. (You can turn around and retrace your steps here or turn right at intersection 7 and right again at intersection 3 to loop back to the parking area.) This smooth, grassy path cuts across a series of fields, beginning with a currently maintained meadow and ending with a field now completely overgrown with trees and shrubs. The stone walls bordering many of the meadows remind hikers of the former uses of this land. You can teach even the youngest children important environmental lessons with a game of "What if everyone did it?" What if, for instance, everyone stepped off the trail, chased the birds, dropped gum wrappers along the way, or picked flowers? One mile from the start, at intersection 11, turn left onto the Fifth Pasture Trail.

Once you have crossed Fifth Pasture, a domed meadow near the southernmost point of the sanctuary, a right turn at intersection 15 and a left-hand turn at junction 13 just 0.5 mile later will return you to the P trail. What kind of animals probably live at the sanctuary? Each child can pretend to be an animal (an animal in motion, of course) and the others can take turns guessing what kind of animal he or she is. Some suggestions: a bullfrog, goldfish (in Wildlife Pond), a woodpecker, an otter, or a snowshoe hare. At intersection 9, turn left, continuing to follow the Pasture Trail for another 0.4 mile to a dirt road where the trail bends to the right and continues for 0.6 mile to the parking area and sanctuary headquarters.

Notes: Picnics are allowed only in designated areas; dogs are forbidden. A moderate admission per person is charged. Closed Mondays; open dawn to dusk. During a wet spring, the boardwalk may be partially submerged. Call ahead or wear high, waterproof footgear.

A peek into the swamp from along Wachusett Meadow's half-mile boardwalk

46. Wachusett Mountain

Type: Dayhike
Difficulty: Moderate for children
Distance: 3 miles, round trip
Hiking time: 2.5 hours
High point/elevation gain: 2006 feet, 700 feet
Hikable: May–November
Maps: USGS Wachusett Mountain

While kids might not grasp the full impact of a view stretching 140 miles to Mount Washington, most will delight in the top-of-the-world feeling as they survey the countryside from the Wachusett summit, the highest point in central Massachusetts. This is not a difficult mountain to climb by New England standards, but it is a mountain just the same, and the steady upward nature of this hike makes it a challenge for everyone. Proper footwear is a must. If you hike in early spring, you can stop for a snack on the crest while you watch the skiers arriving by chair lift to begin their "swoosh" down the slopes. A spring or fall hike (on a warm, sunny day) will most likely offer you an opportunity to watch kettles of migrating hawks soaring high over the valley.

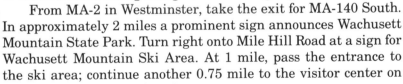

From MA-2 in Westminster, take the exit for MA-140 South. In approximately 2 miles a prominent sign announces Wachusett Mountain State Park. Turn right onto Mile Hill Road at a sign for Wachusett Mountain Ski Area. At 1 mile, pass the entrance to the ski area; continue another 0.75 mile to the visitor center on the right-hand side and park.

Begin your hike at the far right corner of the parking area following the triangular blue blazes of the Bicentennial Trail. The trail heads south, traveling along the base of the mountain. At 0.2 mile, pass the Pine Hill Trail on the right; the Bicentennial Trail continues slightly left. Two-tenths of a mile later, turn right (west) onto the rock-strewn Loop Trail. At a spur about one-half mile from the start, southeasterly views of the surrounding farmland and distant Worcester hills begin to emerge. Listen for the tapping of woodpeckers. Climb steeply and steadily to a junction with Mountain House Trail which continues to the mountaintop. Continue following blue triangular blazes and stay to the right as

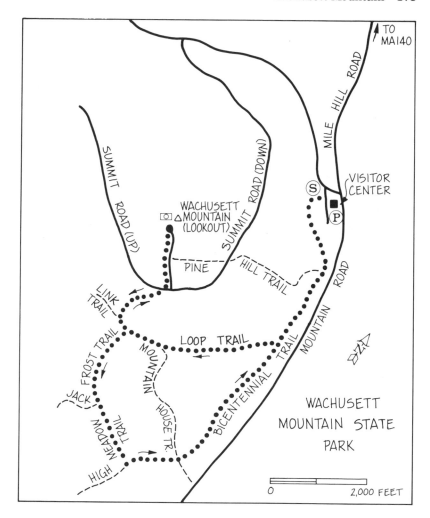

the Jack Frost and Link trails join the Mountain House Trail from the left. Climbing up this rugged path is much like mounting an extended flight of stairs. Children will need one or two rest stops along this stretch because the ascent is continuous. Just before the summit, cross the auto road and head back into the woods. Continue to an outlook and observation tower at the mountaintop, 1.2 miles from the start. On a clear day, the Boston skyline is visible 50 miles due east. To the northwest, look for Mount Monadnock; to the north, Mount Washington, some 140 miles distant.

An energy break atop Wachusett Mountain

To complete the loop, follow the Mountain House Trail back to the junction with the Jack Frost Trail. Take the Jack Frost Trail right (south) and it quickly becomes relatively level, reaching a secondary summit in 0.2 mile. Here, join the High Meadow Trail on the left (southeast) and descend for 0.15 mile over the steepest terrain thus far. After a stretch on flatter ground, the Bicentennial Trail joins from the left. Take this even, meandering trail nearly 1 mile back to your car.

47. Mount Watatic

Type: Dayhike
Difficulty: Moderate for children
Distance: 2.3 miles, loop
Hiking time: 2.5 hours
High point/elevation gain: 1832 feet, 650 feet
Hikable: April–November
Maps: USGS Ashburnham

A not-too-tough climb to the top of Mount Watatic in Ashburnham State Forest will give kids the opportunity to do some safe summit exploring (there is no danger of them toppling off a cliff) while adults take in the four-state panoramic view. Two different return routes give kids and parents a choice between a steep descent and a more gradual one.

From the junction of MA-101 and MA-119 in Ashburnham, travel west for 1.4 miles on MA-119 and park in the area off the road on the right.

At the far end of the parking area, a sign for the Wapack Trail and Mount Watatic leads hikers onto a level jeep road marked by yellow triangular blazes and bordered by stone walls. After passing a small pond surrounded by hemlocks, the trail climbs more steeply. A sign pointing the way to the the Wapack Trail (0.6 mile away) leads to a right turn through a stone wall as the jeep trail continues straight. A second sign indicates that this trail is called the Blueberry Ledges Trail. The blue-blazed route fords a stream and squeezes between two halves of an elephant-sized boulder. Just 0.25 mile into the hike, the trail winds steeply through a hemlock grove and turns right. After a 0.3-mile ascent, the path breaks into an open area with good views to the west and northwest of Mount Monadnock.

Continuing along a high ridge, several trailside spots offer good places to stop and enjoy lunch or a snack. The trail heads through a stone wall, away from the ridge and into a hemlock forest. First gradually, then more sharply, the trail threads its way to the summit of Mount Watatic. Less than a mile from the start, the Blueberry Ledges Trail ends as the yellow-blazed Wapack Trail enters from the left. Continue your southeasterly climb. Soon after passing a shelter, the fire tower comes into view. Although the tower is closed, it's hard to imagine that the views could be much better than those from ground level. The Boston skyline is visible to the east, the Vermont mountains to the northwest, and to the west, the Adirondacks and Mount Greylock. To return to your car, you can follow the yellow blazes on a very steep, wide 0.5-mile descent to the highway, then turn right and walk 0.7 mile to your car. Older children might enjoy the challenge of the downward scramble. (Or you can reverse your steps to follow a more gradual route and avoid the highway walk, a better choice, perhaps, for younger kids.)

48. Purgatory Chasm

Type: Dayhike
Difficulty: Moderate for children
Distance: 1 mile, round trip
Hiking time: 2 hours
High point/elevation gain: 550 feet, 140 feet
Hikable: May–November
Maps: USGS Grafton

If ever a geological fault was created with kids in mind, this is it. Purgatory Chasm is a lengthy gorge some 60 feet wide with sheer walls rising 70 feet high. As you wind your way through the maze of boulders lining the chasm floor, squeezing through small caves and channels with spooky names like "Devil's Coffin" and "Devil's Pulpit," you may pause to watch a rock climber inching his or her way up the chasm wall. Families with small children may need a good deal of time and effort to get from one end of the gorge to the other, but you will enjoy every minute. You will no doubt meet a number of other folks following the same trail but somehow, on this adventure, it doesn't matter. In fact, it's fun to trade incredulous comments with other, equally awestruck people. On the return trip, you will view the gorge from perhaps a more breathtaking perspective—from above.

 From the junction of US 20 and MA-146 in Millbury, take MA-146 south for 7.2 miles to Purgatory Road. Turn right (west) onto Purgatory Road and drive 0.4 mile to the second parking area, which is on the left side of the road near the picnic pavilion.

Follow the blue blazes the length of the gorge (although you don't need to remain on the designated trail because you can't get lost and there is little vegetation to be disturbed). Remain close to younger children who will need almost constant assistance squeezing between piles of boulders and scaling others. Don't allow the inevitably slow pace to annoy you. There is so much to see and so many hollows and tunnels to explore that children are likely to forget that this is a hike. As you exit the chasm, continue straight on the path, ignoring the "Trail" sign that indicates a right- or left-hand turn. Soon, the route splits; head left (east) and walk less than 0.3 mile on a wooded path to a fork. Turn left

Rappelling into Purgatory Chasm

(north), heading back toward the chasm. The blazes will lead you along the edge of the cliffs. Side trips for better views into the gorge can be made with care. Just 1 mile from the start, you will return to the parking area. (You can alter the return trip by eliminating the woods walk and following the "Trail" sign to travel the entire route along the edge of the cliff. But this is not advisable for adults hiking with small children. They should opt for the wooded path since this section of trail does not necessitate constant supervision of the kids.)

49. Drumlin Farm Wildlife Sanctuary

Type: Dayhike
Difficulty: Easy for children
Distance: 2 miles, round trip
Hiking time: 1 to 2 hours
High point/elevation gain: 285 feet, 100 feet
Hikable: Year-round
Maps: USGS Concord

Drumlin Farm Wildlife Sanctuary, headquarters for the Massachusetts Audubon Society, is a 200-acre preserve with exhibits of wild and domestic animals common to the state: hawks, eagles, owls, vultures, foxes, cows, sheep, goats, and pigs. Don't expect to embark on a strenuous hike here; rather plan to enjoy a stroll through a small zoo followed by a walk through the woods punctuated by stops at child-sized observation platforms. Although you may find it a little crowded on warm weekends, Drumlin Farm will be a favorite with everyone from the toddler to Great Grandpa. You'll definitely plan a return trip.

 From the east, take US 20 (Exit 49 off MA-128) 0.3 mile east to MA-117 West. From MA-117 West, drive approximately 6 miles, past the Codman Road fork, to the sanctuary entrance. From the west, at the intersection of MA-117 and MA-126, travel east on MA-117 for 0.7 mile and turn right into Drumlin Farm. Bear right inside the gates to park in the public parking area.

From the Allen Morgan Center (where you pay a moderate admission fee per person; children under 3 are free), walk down the wide, paved road to intersection 2, where you bear left onto Bird Hill Trail, passing a number of wild bird exhibits (rest rooms are along this path). Follow this trail as it veers eastward to intersection 5; turn right and then right again up the side of a small hill past several owl displays. Head left at intersection 3 and walk straight on the Farmyard Trail toward the Sheep and Goat Shed, then wind around the field to the Pig Pen and the Poultry House. In season, a garden across from the Poultry House yields food for the animals as well as demonstrates organic gardening techniques and produces vegetables for sale.

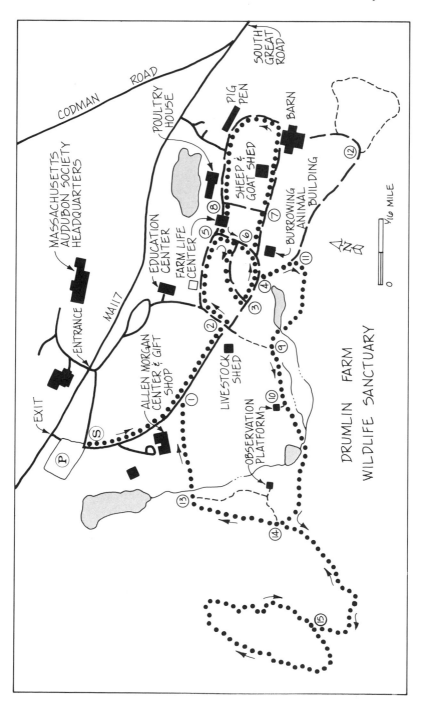

Back at intersection 5, turn left and shortly turn right at junction 6 (here the kids will surely want to visit the underground Burrowing Animal Building). At intersection 4, you will head left onto Deer Trail, a path that leads into the woods past a large deer pen to join Pond View Trail at junction 9. This route skirts a small marshy pond with a couple of small observation platforms before joining the Drumlin Trail. At junction 14, turn left. Although it's unlikely you'll get lost, remember that blue trail markings lead away from the parking area and yellow ones lead back toward it. Stay on this wide path to intersection 15. Turn in either direction to travel a loop that climbs the drumlin (where you may catch sight of a soaring hawk) and then returns you to junction 15. Follow the "D" Trail back to intersection number 1, which joins the paved road that you followed at the very beginning of your walk. You will probably be unable to resist taking another trip past the animal cages and pens before you leave.

Notes: The farm is open year-round and closed Mondays. Picnic in designated areas; no fires. Dogs are not allowed.

Face to face with a recuperating deer at Drumlin Farm

50. Great Blue Hill

Type: Dayhike
Difficulty: Moderate for children
Distance: 2 miles, loop
Hiking time: 2.25 hours
High point/elevation gain: 635 feet, 550 feet
Hikable: April–November
Maps: USGS Blue Hills

Climbing to the summit of Great Blue Hill has been popular since colonial days, although there are quite a few more hikers today than there were 200 years ago. Bostonians flock to the 6500-acre Blue Hills Reservation with its 400 miles of trails; it is the largest undeveloped parcel of land within 35 miles of Boston. The route described here entails a moderately challenging ascent with a rewarding view of the city from atop the summit's stone tower. Kids will thrill to the rocky scramble down the mountain while adults scan the tremendous vistas on the upper portion of the descent for familiar landmarks. After the hike, stop by Houghtons Pond (also part of the reservation) for a swim and picnic supper.

Off of MA-128/I-93, take Exit 2B to MA-138. (As you exit the highway, Great Blue Hill looms nearby.) Take MA-138 North to the first traffic light. Turn right onto Hillside Street. Continue past an intersection with a sign for Houghtons Pond, and, nearly one mile from MA-138, turn left into a parking lot.

Before you begin hiking, you may want to refer to the large trail map at the rear of the parking area. Bear right out of the parking lot on the unblazed Coon Hollow Path. Almost immediately you will bear left at an unmarked intersection; the narrow Coon Hollow Path has become a wide wooded path, marked occasionally with numbered wooden plaques: "1126." Begin a rocky, rugged yet gradual ascent. Don't let the kids start off at too fast a pace or they will wear out quickly. Teach them how to conserve their energy for the strenuous climb ahead. You will pass several trail intersections within the first 0.4 mile including the blue-blazed South Skyline Trail on which you will return. A trail

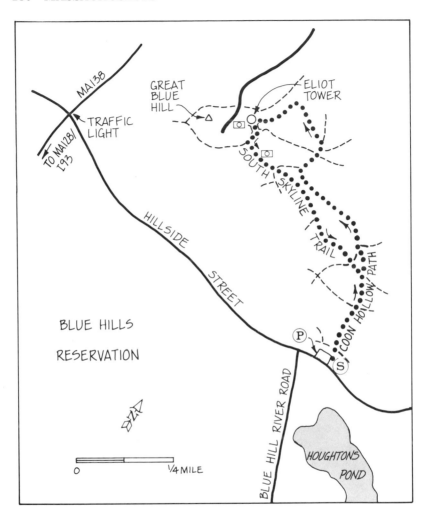

marked with fluorescent green circles soon joins your trail and you follow left on this Five Corners Path. As the green-blazed trail meets a blue-blazed one, bear right; 0.1 mile later, bear left onto a well-worn trail as the green-blazed route heads right. (This trail is blazed with red circles that are only visible if viewed from the opposite direction.) Though well-traveled paths are easy to follow, they make stepping rough on little feet since rocks and roots are more exposed.

One mile from the start, this trail delivers you near the top of

These young hikers on top of Blue Hill have discovered that sandwiches taste even better after you've climbed a mountain!

Great Blue Hill at Eliot Tower with its commanding views of the Boston skyline and the Atlantic Ocean. What kinds of animals can the kids find in the clouds? After gazing at the city from the tower's upper floor and visiting with other hiking families, locate the blue-blazed route traversing a stone bridge. Shortly after crossing the bridge, a granite post on your left and wooden post on the right indicate your left-hand turn onto a steep, rocky, blue-blazed path known as South Skyline Trail. The southern views as you descend via this path are tremendous, perhaps even better than those from the summit. The trail follows a gurgling stream and travels through some interesting boulder fields, with several other trails splitting off to either side along the route. At the fourth trail junction (0.6 mile from the tower), turn right onto the unblazed Coon Hollow Path and follow it for 0.3 mile to your car. If you decide to picnic on the reservation, note that no open fires are allowed (use of grills or fuel stoves is permitted in designated areas only) and no camping. Dogs must be leashed. The reservation closes at 8:00 p.m.

51. World's End Reservation

Type: Dayhike
Difficulty: Easy for children
Distance: 4 miles, loop
Hiking time: 3 hours
High point/elevation gain: 70 feet, 120 feet
Hikable: Year-round
Maps: USGS Hull

World's End, a figure-eight-shaped peninsula dividing Hingham Harbor and the Weir River, is well known for its spectacular topography and landscaping. Families have enjoyed hiking its tree-lined gravel roads and admiring its dramatic glacial drumlins since the turn of the century. In the late 1800s, the property nearly became a planned community with more than 150 homesites, but instead was farmed and then turned into a private park. Three-quarters of a century later, it was again threatened by development. The public rallied and raised $450,000, enabling The Trustees of Reservations to buy the 251-acre parcel and make it available for public enjoyment. If you look across the bay toward Hull at the clusters of homes vying for ocean views and beach frontage, you will appreciate the peaceful, natural setting of World's End. Kids will lead the way on the wide gravel and grass paths that skirt and traverse the drumlins and delight in the constant ocean views.

 From MA-3 in Quincy, take MA-3A to East Hingham. At a rotary, MA-3A heads right; continue straight on a four-lane highway for 0.5 mile to Four Corners. Turn left here onto Martin's Lane and drive 0.7 mile to the reservation parking area. .

The trail that begins at the corner of the parking area farthest from the road is, like the other trails here, unblazed and unnamed, but obvious. At each junction, keep to the right. Soon after entering the woods, a huge rock outcrop on the left will challenge your agile little climbers. After 0.5 mile, the wide trail splits and a side trail takes you to Rocky Neck where, at the tip, the road narrows into a foot trail that leads back to the main path. With the Weir River on your right, the cart path travels along the base of open, grassy Planter's Hill on your left. It may be impossible to keep kids on the trail with the neatly mown fields begging them to break into an aimless run, but warn them first about poison ivy.

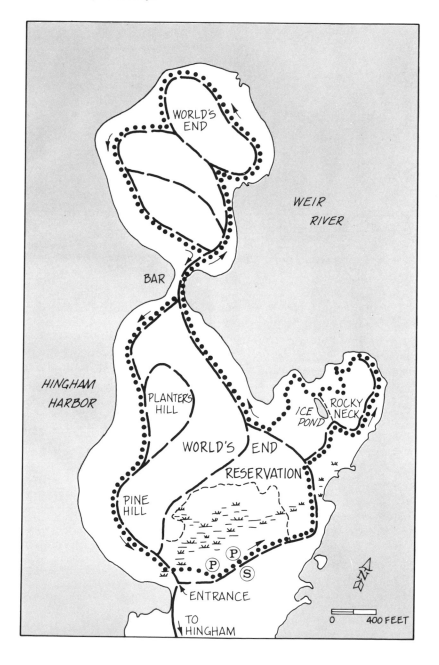

View from the second drumlin, looking back at the connecting sand bar.

Continue 0.3 mile to the sand bar connecting the two drumlins. Here, the stiff ocean breeze will be welcome on a sultry August day and not-so-welcome on a raw day in March. Who will be the first to see the Boston skyline? Travel the perimeter of the outer drumlin, continuing to choose the right-hand path at any trail junctures. As you walk along the eastern side of the peninsula, look beyond Hull and you will see the open Atlantic Ocean. After a 1.2-mile hike, you will return to the sandbar. Cross over to the inner parcel and stay to the right, circling Planter's Hill from the other side with Hingham Harbor on your right. Look for signs of foxes and rabbits and watch for quail, pheasant, and the numerous varieties of sea and shore birds that frequent the area. After an easy climb over Pine Hill, the path will bring you back to the entrance and parking area.

Notes: A moderate admission is charged for persons 16 and older. The reservation opens at 10:00 a.m. and closes at sunset. Picnicking and wading are prohibited.

52. Ipswich River Wildlife Sanctuary

Type:	Dayhike (camping at sanctuary by permit only)
Difficulty:	Easy for children
Distance:	3 miles, loop
Hiking time:	2 hours
High point/elevation gain:	110 feet, 50 feet
Hikable:	April–November
Maps:	USGS Georgetown

The good news: The sanctuary's famed Rockery, a series of stone stairways, tunnels, and bridges built by the property's wealthy owners nearly a century ago, will make this hike unforgettable for the kids. The bad news: once they begin exploring this intricate maze of precisely placed boulders, they may want to end the hike right there! But it's well worth whatever cajoling it may take to get them to continue. Within the sanctuary's 2400 acres are more than 20 miles of hiking trails with features nearly as enticing: boardwalks, rustic bridges, wildflower gardens, and unusual oriental trees and plants. You may even meet up with a snake or a turtle.

From the junction of US 1 and MA-97 in Topsfield, drive southeast on MA-97 for 0.5 mile to Perkins Row, on the left. Turn here and in 1.0 mile turn right, following signs into the Audubon Society property. The parking lot is 0.2 mile from the Perkins Row turnoff on the left.

Borrow a trail map at the information center where you will also pay a moderate admission fee per person. From the parking area, head north across an open field. At the right-hand corner of the field, the trail enters the woods on a slight descent. At junction 20, 0.2 mile into the hike, continue straight on the Rockery ("R") Trail. Do the same at junction 24. Bear left at junction 25, heading for the Rockery, and cross a bridge before veering to the right skirting Rockery Pond. When you arrive at the Rockery at 0.3 mile, encourage the kids to explore all the paths and tunnels, pausing atop the stone structure for a view of Rockery Pond. Imagine hauling these rocks from miles away by horse and cart! Not surprisingly, it took nine years to build this rock master-

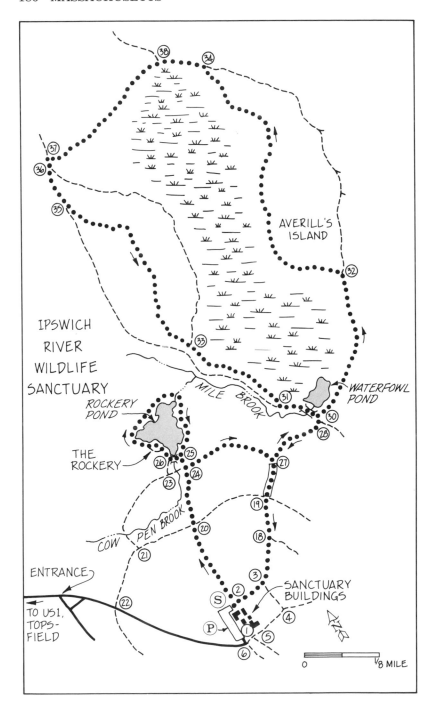

AVERILL'S
ISLAND

IPSWICH
RIVER
WILDLIFE
SANCTUARY

WATERFOWL
POND

ROCKERY
POND

MILE BROOK

THE
ROCKERY

COW PEN BROOK

ENTRANCE

TO US1,
TOPS-
FIELD

SANCTUARY
BUILDINGS

0   ⅛ MILE

piece. Circle the pond (with the water on your right) still on the R Trail. Can you hear bullfrogs calling or make out ducks floating on the still water? Bear left at trail junctions 25 and 24, heading away from the pond along the Waterfowl Pond ("W") Trail. At junction 27, you can turn right to cross a boardwalk and follow the Innermost ("I") Trail back to your car or you can bear left to continue the hike. In nearly 1 mile, you will see the stone bridge that spans Mile Brook near junctions 28 and 30. Pause to look out over Waterfowl Pond. Bear right here, heading for Averill's Is-

The Rockery tunnels at the Ipswich River Wildlife Sanctuary

land on the Averill's Island ("A") Trail. Bear left 0.25 mile later at junction 32, skirting the marsh on your left. In 0.5 mile, bear left again at junction 34; soon after, turn left once more at number 38 to join the White Pine ("P") Trail. At junction 37, bear left, walking now in a southerly direction. Stay to the right at number 36, on the Mile Brook ("M") Trail for less than 0.1 mile and bear left onto the North Esker ("N") Trail at 35. On this path, you walk along a ridge with good views of the wetlands to the east and west. Bearing right at 33 and left at 31 will bring you back to the stone bridge. By turning right at the bridge, left at 27 on the boardwalk (always a favorite), and heading straight through the number 19 intersection, you will reach junction 18, just 0.1 mile from your car. Stay to the right and do the same at junction 3 to return to the Audubon buildings and parking area.

Notes: No dogs or fires. Picnic only in designated areas. Closed Mondays.

53. Parker River National Wildlife Refuge

Type: Dayhike
Difficulty: Easy for children
Distance: 3 miles, loop
Hiking time: 2.5 hours
High point/elevation gain: 40 feet, 40 feet
Hikable: April–October
Maps: USGS Ipswich

The 4662-acre Parker River National Wildlife Refuge, covering two-thirds of Plum Island, offers several different nature trails that traverse barren sand dunes, lush marshes, and glacial drumlins. Sandy Point State Reservation lies at the southernmost tip of the island. Plum Island is a favorite spot for birdwatchers—nearly 300 species of birds frequent the area—as well as sunbathers who have learned that by arriving early they can secure some of the few parking spaces inside the refuge. Often, on a hot summer's day, the gates are closed and the parking lot full

The isolated, rocky beach of the Parker River Wildlife Refuge

by 8:00 a.m. The benefit of this policy to the seaside hiker is relative seclusion: Where else within 30 miles of Boston can the children virtually own seven miles of unspoiled beach for the afternoon? Hiking during the warm months requires sunscreen, bathing suits, towels, pails, and shovels. (There are no lifeguards; warn children who wish to swim about strong undertows.) If you visit the refuge between the Tuesday after Labor Day and October 31, you can pick up to one quart of plums or cranberries. (Avoid the refuge during hunting season—late fall through winter.) A moderate admission to the refuge is charged per car.

    From US 1 in Newbury, turn onto Hanover Street (just south of the Newburyport/Newbury border) where a sign indicates that Plum Island is 4 miles away. In less than 1 mile, go straight through the intersection with MA-1A and turn right onto the Water Street/Plum Island Turnpike where a sign directs you to the Parker River National Wildlife Refuge. Shortly after crossing the bridge to Plum Island, turn right onto Sunset Drive (following another sign) and drive to the refuge gate. Continue 6.5 miles to parking lot 7.

    Before starting the hike, you may want to view the ocean and southern Plum Island from the observation tower adjacent to lot 7. The walk begins on a boardwalk close to the parking lot that leads to the Atlantic Ocean. Turn right and continue along the sandy shore. At a row of boulders, Parker River ends and Sandy Point begins. Just beyond this marker, the rocky drumlin known as Bar Head rises above the ocean. Along the path, marked by white-blazed stakes, there are some steep dropoffs to the beach area, but nothing that should cause parents alarm. The rugged terrain of Bar Head concedes to sand once more as you walk toward Sandy Point. The kids will probably be unable to resist kicking off their shoes and wading in the cool water.

At the point, turn and head north along a vast stretch of untarnished beach. If the kids have tired of wading or watching the waves come and go, have them scan the sand dunes for signs of long-destroyed summer cottages. One and seven-tenths of a mile from the start, you will arrive at a fence marking the perimeter of the refuge. Turn right here and, in less than 30 yards, turn right again onto a dirt road. This path will take you past a freshwater swamp on the outskirts of Stage Island Pool. Do the children see any signs of muskrats? After walking along the road for 0.5 mile, you will go through a gate and across a parking area. A trail winds through thick scrub, once again climbing atop Bar Head (watch out for poison ivy.) The trail leaves the woods and descends to the beach, turning left and leading to a boardwalk. Head through a parking area and continue along a dirt road to lot 7 where you parked your car.

---

54. Sandy Neck

Type: Dayhike
Difficulty: Difficult for children
Distance: 4 miles, loop
Hiking time: 4 hours
High point/elevation gain: 40 feet, 100 feet
Hikable: Year-round
Maps: USGS Hyannis

Sandy Neck on Cape Cod is a 6-mile-long coastal barrier beach that offers hiking trails that follow along the isolated shore, wind among sculptured sand dunes, and wander past the

Relaxing on the beaches of Sandy Neck

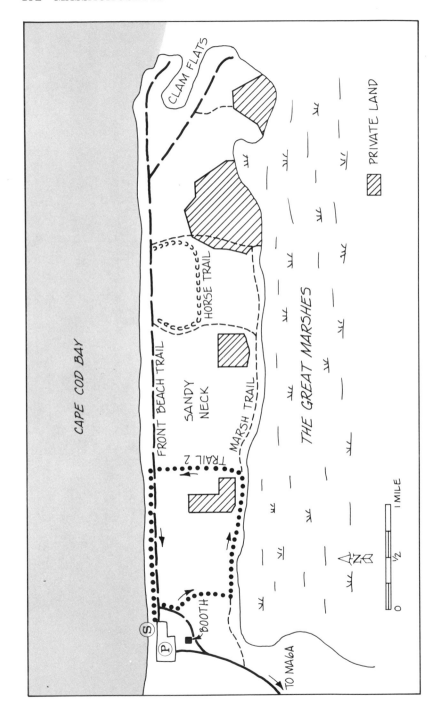

CLAM FLATS

PRIVATE LAND

HORSE TRAIL

FRONT BEACH TRAIL

SANDY NECK

MARSH TRAIL

TRAIL 2

THE GREAT MARSHES

CAPE COD BAY

BOOTH

TO MA6A

N

1 MILE

½

0

lush Great Marshes. Due to the loose nature of the sandy soil, walking is arduous and this is a hike for those in very good physical condition. Arrive early to take advantage of the morning coolness (or hike during the cooler seasons) and don't forget to bring water, sunscreen, and hats for everyone. A book to identify animal tracks in the sand will turn the kids' attention away from their hot, tired feet.

From US 6 in Barnstable take Exit 5 and travel north on MA-149. In 1 mile, at the junction with MA-6A in West Barnstable, turn left (west). In another 2 miles, turn right onto Sandy Neck Road. Drive just over 1 mile (passing the parking lot for town residents) and arrive at a beachside parking area.

Descend a flight of steps to the beach and turn right. Walk along the water's edge until you see a sign for four-wheel drive vehicles; turn right. In 100 yards, on the left there is a signpost warning vehicles to watch for hikers crossing the road. Turn left at this signpost and follow the trail into the dunes. As the trail winds among these sandy knolls, it becomes indistinct at times because footsteps head off in all directions. But because of the fragile nature of this seaside environment, it is important to locate and stick to the marked trails. Head for the edge of the Great Marshes and use the orange markers to guide you along Marsh Trail. In the soft, windswept sand watch for bird, deer, and rabbit tracks. The trail skirts several dwellings and arrives at a sign for Trail 2 at 2 miles. Turn left (north) here between impressive dunes and soon arrive at Cape Cod Bay. Turn left (west) onto Front Beach Trail which follows along the water. Here the kids can break into a run along the firmer beach sand, dodging the playful waves. This would be a great time to take an energy break. Lie back and relax, pointing out the shapes created by the puffy, drifting clouds overhead. (We always manage to find a galloping horse and a hippo with its mouth open.)

Continuing the hike, after about 1 mile, you will see the sign for Trail 1 pointing toward the dunes. Continue walking along the water for another 0.25 mile to the parking area. If it's warm enough, grab your bathing suits and dive into the waves.

55. Seaside Trail

Type: Dayhike
Difficulty: Easy for children
Distance: 2.4 miles, loop
Hiking time: 2.5 hours
High point/elevation gain: 50 feet, 50 feet
Hikable: Year-round
Maps: USGS Chatham

Long ago, folks in Chatham worked in the shipbuilding, fishing, and whaling industries. Today, they cater to the tourists who arrive at Cape Cod in droves each summer. If you want to take advantage of all of the hot-weather fun offered on the Cape and don't mind crowds and traffic, visit in July or August. If you prefer more solitude, schedule your trip for just after Labor Day (or before Memorial Day, though it's likely you'll encounter rain). The hike described here on the Seaside Trail and along Harding Beach offers kids opportunities for wading, kite flying, or collecting. What will be the treasure of the day—the abandoned shell of a horseshoe crab, a piece of driftwood shaped like a galloping horse, or a smooth stone of a favorite color?

From the rotary in Chatham center, drive 1.7 miles west on MA-28 North. At the blinking light, turn left onto Barn Hill Road. In 0.4 mile, bear right at the fork onto Harding Beach Road, which leads to the parking lot entrance (pay a small parking fee in season). Head left along the edge of the parking area past a building into the smaller parking lot and leave your car.

The trail begins at the corner of the parking lot closest to the water. Hike along this sandy road for just over half a mile with various side trails offering closer looks at the ocean. Keep curious children from wandering among the dunes since this is a nesting area for birds such as the horned lark. After a long, gradual ascent, you will be able to see across the salt marshes and Oyster Pond River to the left and Nantucket Sound to the right. At about the 1-mile mark, you arrive at a fork with a private residence on your left. Bear right and continue to follow the road to a water-

The Seaside Trail is ideal for toddlers.

way leading out of Stage Harbor. The flat boulders lining the waterway make a good spot to rest and watch the procession of boats chugging through the channel. On your return trip, follow along the shore of Harding Beach for 1 mile. Enjoy wading, swimming, or chasing the tireless waves before heading home.

56. Fort Hill Trail

Type: Dayhike
Difficulty: Easy for children
Distance: 1.5 miles, loop
Hiking time: 2 hours
High point/elevation gain: 50 feet, 100 feet
Hikable: Year-round
Maps: USGS Orleans

As you walk the Fort Hill Trail, part of the Cape Cod National Seashore, you will realize that Cape Cod is more than sand dunes, clam rolls, and lighthouses. Featuring a boardwalk through wetlands, two small hill climbs with views over Nauset Marsh, historic Indian Rock, and a stroll around the grounds of whaleship captain Edward Penniman's historic home, these trails offer a distinct vision of the Cape.

From the junction of US 6 and MA-28 (at a rotary) on the Eastham/Orleans border, drive north on US 6 for 1.2 miles to a right turn onto Governor Prence Road. Make another right turn onto Fort Hill Road and drive to the parking area on the left marked with a Fort Hill sign.

Begin on the trail that leads into the woods from the right (eastern) side of the parking lot. Head uphill on rustic steps through the forest peppered with black locust trees. Soon, you will leave the woods and walk along the edge of a large field that abuts Nauset Marsh. Stone walls that once marked farmers' boundaries remind hikers of the former uses of this land. Partway into the field, at 0.1 mile, turn left into the woods followed immediately by another left. Walk along the Red Maple Swamp Trail, bearing right in 0.3 mile to follow a series of boardwalks (little ones can try to keep count) through Red Maple Swamp. There's something about boardwalks that kids love—they are easy to follow and fun to run on.

At an intersection about 0.6 mile into the hike, turn right to follow the trail another 0.2 mile to a paved path where another right turn at close to 1 mile will bring you first to an overlook of the bay and the distant Atlantic Ocean and then to a pavilion housing Indian Rock. Encourage kids to examine this boulder

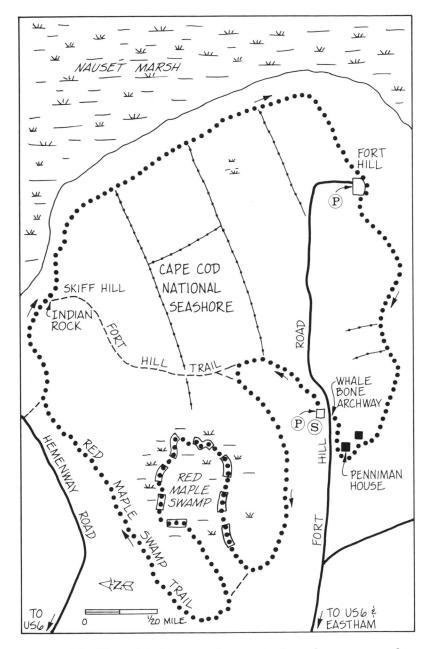

once used by Nauset Indians to sharpen tools and weapons and to shape fish hooks. From the back of the pavilion take the Fort Hill Trail to the left; the trail skirts the marsh's edge. Hike for about

The unique whalebone archway in front of the Penniman House

0.4 mile to Fort Hill and another parking area. Enjoy the views over the marsh before continuing on this trail another 0.3 mile to the Penniman House. You will travel behind the buildings, through the front yard, and pass under the whalebone archway at the edge of the Penniman property. Such magnificent entryways date back to the days when whaling was big business on the Cape. Your car is in the parking lot diagonally across the street to the right.

57. The Nauset Marsh Trail

Type: Dayhike
Difficulty: Easy for children
Distance: 1.25 miles, loop
Hiking time: 2 hours
High point/elevation gain: 60 feet, 90 feet
Hikable: Year-round
Maps: USGS Orleans

The Cape is constantly changing due to natural forces such as fierce ocean storms and the pounding surf as well as human encroachment and development. Near Wellfleet, the Cape has eroded to only 1 mile wide and, in Provincetown, giant dunes threaten to overtake the highway. On the Nauset Marsh Trail, which is part of the Cape Cod National Seashore, you will witness some of the natural change affecting the Cape as the tides swell and then flush the pond and marsh areas at precise intervals. This is a super walk for young families, just over 1 mile long with a variety of water views. Watch out for poison ivy, which grows rampant on the Cape. Sneakers are fine.

Drive north on US 6 past the rotary at the Orleans/Eastham town line. Slow down at mile marker 94. At mile 94.282, turn right onto Doane Road (also called Nauset Road) into the Salt Pond Visitors Center approximately 3 miles beyond the rotary.

The hike begins near the Salt Pond Visitors Center to the right of the outdoor amphitheater. The sandy trail, initially sprinkled with crushed white shells, quickly drops to the shore of Salt Pond and follows along the water's edge on a wide gravel path. Salt Pond was a freshwater "kettle pond" until the ocean waters spilled over from Nauset Marsh long ago and a thin channel was created linking the marsh and pond. Today, Salt Pond nurtures a wide variety of marine creatures, some swept in and out by the twice-daily tides. Can the kids spot any sandpipers? These small birds with grayish-brown backs and white bellies eat the aquatic insects and small crustaceans that they find in or near Salt Pond.

Head through the woods and up a low hill on a series of steps to an overlook 0.6 mile from the start. Just below the overlook lies

Salt Pond Bay, with Nauset Beach to the east and Nauset Harbor beyond the marsh flats to the east-southeast. After you have enjoyed the lovely views and the sounds of the ocean birds, follow the path as it skirts the marsh and then curls to the left through airy woodlands. The eastern red cedar stands replaced the golf course that stretched along the marsh in the early 1900s. The trail crosses a bike path and then plunges into denser forest with frequent placards pointing out varieties of trees and plants. After crossing the bike path a second time, the Nauset Trail joins the Buttonbush Trail, which heads in two directions. Bear left. The Buttonbush Trail is a self-guided nature trail that has been adapted for use by handicapped and blind visitors. A short walk along this path will complete the loop and return you to the Salt Pond Visitors Center.

Crossing Nauset Marsh

58. Great Island Trail

Type: Dayhike
Difficulty: Difficult for children
Distance: 6 miles, round trip
Hiking time: 5 hours
High point/elevation gain: 75 feet, 150 feet
Hikable: Year-round
Maps: USGS Wellfleet

Come to Great Island, one of the Cape Cod National Seashore sites, early in the morning with sun hats, sunscreen, canteens, and rugged hiking boots. The trail circles a salt marsh, winds through pitch pine forests, climbs over towering dunes, and finishes along an extensive stretch of Cape Cod Bay beach. If you intend to extend this from a 6-mile to an 8.4-mile round trip hike by walking out to Jeremy Point, make sure you will arrive at the connecting spit at low and receding tide. Remember that walking on loose sand takes considerable effort and young children may get frustrated at their lack of progress.

On US 6 in Wellfleet (heading toward Provincetown), take the exit for Wellfleet Center and Harbor, 5 miles north of the Wellfleet town line. Turn left off the exit ramp and drive through Wellfleet Center to a left turn onto Chequesset Neck Road at 0.6 mile. At an intersection in 0.4 mile, turn right. At the Town Pier, turn right. Drive 2.3 miles and turn left into Great Island and a large parking area.

The trail of white crushed shells bordered by round logs leaves the left side of the parking lot (which is closed from midnight to 6:00 a.m.), winds through a wooded section, and emerges at the tidal flat near the mouth of the Herring River. The salt hay you see along the path was once a staple in the diet of grazing cattle because of its nutritional value. Turn right at water's edge and begin walking along the sandy road that encircles the tidal flat or "The Gut." Look for signs of ocean life in the sand: gull tracks, fiddler crabs, broken shells. A short, steep boardwalk provides access to the beach on the other side of the dunes. At the end of the tidal flat, as the dunes loom before you, bear left still skirting the marsh, then head right when the trail divides just past

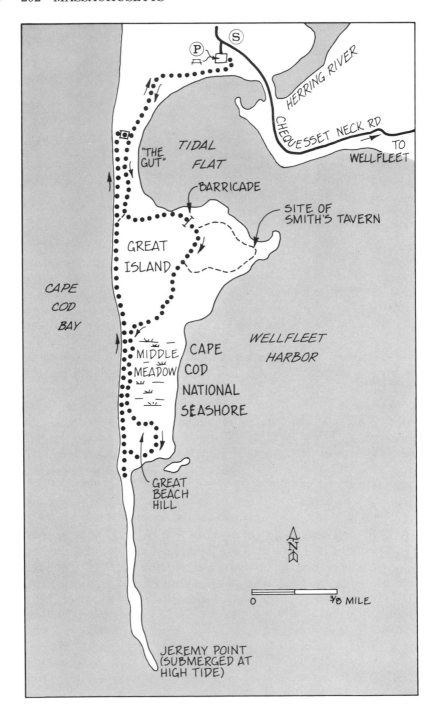

"THE GUT"

TIDAL FLAT

BARRICADE

SITE OF SMITH'S TAVERN

GREAT ISLAND

CAPE COD BAY

WELLFLEET HARBOR

MIDDLE MEADOW

CAPE COD NATIONAL SEASHORE

GREAT BEACH HILL

HERRING RIVER

CHEQUESSET NECK RD.

TO WELLFLEET

JEREMY POINT (SUBMERGED AT HIGH TIDE)

N

0   ⅜ MILE

the barricade to motor vehicles. (A short side trail on the left takes you to the site of the eighteenth-century Smith's Tavern, 1.8 miles from the start.) The narrow, main trail climbs to the summit of Great Island through a cluster of pines and then drops to Middle Meadow. After skirting this marshy area, the path rolls

An easy descent to the beach that wraps around Great Island's "Gut"

over some dunes before climbing Great Beach Hill at 2.8 miles. Enjoy the vast views over Cape Cod Bay. From the southerly base of the hill, Jeremy Point is 1.2 miles away, accessed by a narrow spit. (Be sure that you know the tide schedule before heading to the point. Remember, this will add 2.4 miles to your hike.) You can return by walking along the beach on the Cape Cod Bay side of Great lsland (or, if you prefer to make the hike 0.8 mile longer, by the way you came). If you choose to walk the beach, watch not only for beach "treasures" but also for the boardwalk that will carry you over the dunes to "The Gut." From there, follow along the left of the tidal flat to the wooded path that will return you to the parking area.

59. Cedar Tree Neck Sanctuary

Type: Dayhike
Difficulty: Easy for children
Distance: 2 miles, loop
Hiking time: 2.5 hours
High point/elevation gain: 100 feet, 150 feet
Hikable: Year-round
Maps: USGS Vineyard Haven

The island of Martha's Vineyard, just five miles off of the south shore of Cape Cod, attracted its first permanent white settlers in 1642 and now, nearly 350 years later, welcomes a flood of visitors each summer. You may want to plan your trip for September or October, when the days are still warm enough for outdoor fun but the crowds have returned to the mainland. (By late fall, however, many restaurants, inns, and stores have closed for the season.) The Woods Hole, Martha's Vineyard, and Nantucket Steamship Authority is the only ferry line that carries cars across to the island; the ferry leaves from Woods Hole (on the shoulder of the Cape) for Vineyard Haven or Oak Bluffs. Kids will relish the 45-minute ferry ride, sitting on the breezy open deck and watching the sea gulls, fishing boats, and the approaching island. Call

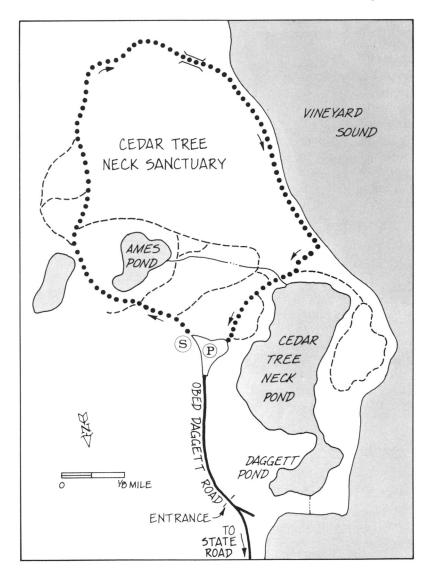

(508)540-2022 for schedules and reservations (which should be made well in advance). The two Vineyard hikes described in this guide center around the north shore, which is more heavily wooded and better suited for hiking; the south shore is more appropriate for oceanside recreation, sunning, swimming, and wading in the rolling surf.

On the beaches of Cedar Tree Neck, shorebirds easily outnumber hikers.

The Cedar Tree Neck Sanctuary, managed by the Sherriff's Meadow Foundation, encompasses a freshwater pond and bog, woodlands, rocky bluffs, and open fields. The easy-to-follow nature trails wind through the forest and along the solitary beach, making it one of the island's most enjoyable walks. Don't forget to bring along a bag for collecting treasures from the seashore.

From the junction of State Road and Edgartown Road in Vineyard Haven, drive southwest on State Road for about 2.5 miles to a fork. Bear right here, remaining on State Road. After a sign for Lambert's Cove at 3.9 miles, in 100 yards bear right onto paved Indian Hill Road. At 1.7 miles, turn right at a sign for Cedar Tree Neck onto a rough, one-lane dirt road (Obed Daggett Road). After 1 mile, you will arrive at the parking area for Cedar Tree Neck.

A detailed wooden map in the parking area shows the color-coded, marked trails that wind through the Cedar Tree Neck preserve. The white trail heads out of the parking area's southeast side and ascends for the first 0.5 mile. The narrow trail squeezes through low shrubbery and mountain laurel and feels more like a trail winding through the foothills of New Hampshire's White Mountains than a path approaching the seashore.

After the initial steady climb, the trail rides up and down hilly terrain to a footbridge over a stream at 1.2 miles and a steep climb to the top of a bluff. On the down side of this hill, the ocean becomes visible. Soon the trail outlets onto one of the most beautiful stretches of beach anywhere. Mother Nature has claimed this shore for her own; white sand, rocks, and ocean birds replace portable radios and volleyball nets here. Since swimming is not allowed here, encourage your young artists to draw giant pictures in the sand with sturdy sticks. Head right, strolling down the beach for approximately 0.4 mile before turning onto the red trail. (Locate this trail by looking between two great dunes for a footpath.) The red trail leaves the beach area and rises into the woods, skirting Cedar Tree Neck Pond. Avoid side trails (blazed with white or yellow) and the red trail will eventually return you to the parking area.

Notes: The sanctuary closes at 5:30 p.m. No swimming, picnicking, or camping.

60. Felix Neck Wildlife Sanctuary

Type: Dayhike
Difficulty: Easy for children
Distance: 1.7 miles, loop
Hiking time: 1.5 hours
High point/elevation gain: 50 feet, 75 feet
Hikable: Year-round
Maps: USGS Edgartown

An Audubon property, the Felix Neck Wildlife Sanctuary on Martha's Vineyard offers 350 acres of marsh, fields, forest, and beach to explore. If you're lucky, the rehabilitation building where oiled birds are treated and young water birds are reared will be occupied. Stop by the barn to visit the exhibit room and library before or after your walk.

From the center of Edgartown, drive 3 miles on Edgartown Vineyard Haven Road. Turn right at a blue-and-white Audubon Society sign and a granite pillar stamped "Felix Neck Wildlife Sanctuary." Travel down a one-lane road (with two-way traffic) for about 0.5 mile to the sanctuary parking area. From Oak Bluffs or Vineyard Haven, travel south on the Edgartown–Vineyard Haven Road 1.2 miles past the intersection with County Road and turn left into the Felix Neck Wildlife Sanctuary.

Pay the small nonmember admission fee per person at the visitors center 100 yards from the parking area. Follow the orange trail (marked by orange-tipped wooden stakes) that heads to the right (east) from the visitors center. Within the first 0.2 mile, you will come to a camera bluff just off the Orange Trail that overlooks Waterfowl Pond. Stop by the observation building and study the poster of various species of waterfowl. How many of these birds can the children see on the pond? Return to the Orange Trail and hike for 0.2 mile to the intersection with the Red Trail near Sengekontacket Pond. Follow the Orange Trail to its completion at water's edge for a pretty view over the pond.

Return to the Orange and Red trails junction and turn right

The waterfowl poster in the Felix Neck observation building will help with bird identification.

here, enjoying lovely water views for 0.3 mile until you head back into the woods. Soon you will cross the Old Road and, 0.9 mile from the start, reach an intersection with the Yellow Trail. Here, turn right, travel past Elizabeth's Pond, and walk the 0.3 mile to the photography blind at the edge of Sengekontacket Pond. If the children aren't too impatient, pause here to see what types of water birds will come close to the photography blind. Retrace your steps along the Yellow Trail, skirting Turtle Pond on the left just

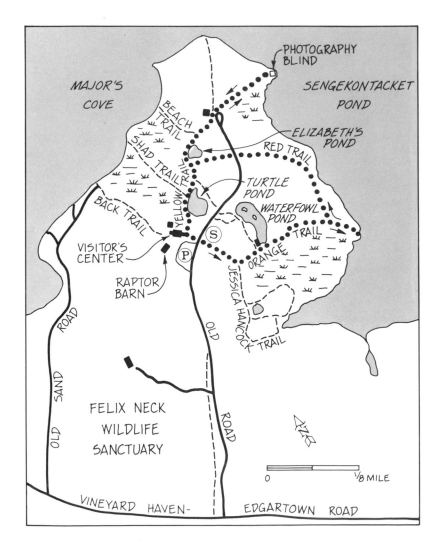

beyond the intersection with the Red Trail. Continue 0.1 mile past the pond to the barn and the nearby parking lot. Keep in mind that the area closes at 7:00 p.m.

Barefeet in the sand at Martha's Vineyard.

RHODE ISLAND

61. Walkabout Trail

Type:	Dayhike or overnight
Difficulty:	Moderate for children
Distance:	6 miles, loop
Hiking time:	3.5 hours
High point/elevation gain:	720 feet, 240 feet
Hikable:	July–December
Maps:	USGS Chepachet and Thompson

The Walkabout Trail (in Burrillville and Glocester), with its 2-, 6-, and 8-mile options, is a good first family hike. The trail markers are bright and easy to follow and the route is level, though rocky and damp in places. If you hike in late summer, the trail will be less muddy, and you can end the day with a swim in Bowdish Reservoir. A plaque imbedded in a rock near the park office tells the story of the Australian sailors who blazed the trail 25 years ago, naming it "walkabout" in reference to the aborigines who wander the Australian countryside.

 From I-395 in Connecticut, take the exit for US 44 East. Travel 6.9 miles on US 44 East to the George Washington Camping Area on the left. Turn left off the highway and drive 0.4 mile to the park office, set back from the road on the left. Turn and park there.

The hike begins on the nature trail where the three loops converge. Walk from the parking area back to the main camp road; on the opposite side, the trail heads northeast into the woods. Follow this path marked with frequent three-colored blazes—orange for the 8-mile hike, red for the 6-mile hike, and blue for the 2-mile loop—as it ambles through the woods. At 0.6 mile, the blue blazes depart left from the orange and red. (The blue-blazed loop is an alternative for families desiring a shorter hike: Follow the blue blazes through the woods, onto a dirt road, back into the forest, and through a picnic and camping area. There it rejoins the longer loops.) The red and orange trails dip into a damp, swampy section where rustic log bridges help hikers traverse the wettest spots. After swinging onto higher ground and crossing a road at 2.2 miles, the trail begins a lengthy stretch through the forest.

At the 3.5-mile mark just after a short uphill, the orange route splits off, heading right. Remain on the red trail, crossing a stream and climbing gradually through a maze of stone walls that once marked a farmer's boundaries. Numerous fallen trees

A wooden sign explains the Walkabout Trail.

will slow you down through this section. Cross a dirt road and re-join the orange trail at 4.5 miles. The two routes wind through soggy woodlands and then skirt the edge of Wilbur Pond for 0.5 mile. At several points of access to the pond, kids can search for frogs, salamanders, and other creatures. After leaving the pond's edge, the trail follows through wetlands with good footbridge crossings. The trail proceeds through a campground where children will enjoy a brief encounter with camping families. After a quick left turn, the path crosses a dirt road and once again merges with the blue-blazed route less than 1 mile from trail's end. The triple blazes take you directly behind some camping areas through more soggy terrain. The final stretch inches along the rocky edge of Bowdish Reservoir with frequent glimpses of the sparkling water. When you emerge from the woods your car will be in sight—and so will the beach.

62. Ben Utter Trail to Stepstone Falls

Type:	Dayhike or overnight (permit required)
Difficulty:	Easy for children
Distance:	3.5 miles, round trip
Hiking time:	2 hours
High point/elevation gain:	287 feet, 150 feet
Hikable:	April–mid-November
Maps:	USGS Voluntown and Hope Valley

While the sight of the river tumbling and spilling down the wide, steplike rocks delights children, the ever-present sound of the cascading water soothes adult ears. The trip to Stepstone Falls via the Ben Utter Trail—lovely any time of the year, but especially appealing on a steamy day or after a rain storm—understandably rates as one of the most popular hikes in the Arcadia Management Area. While it is possible to begin the hike from the falls, it would be anticlimactic to have to walk away

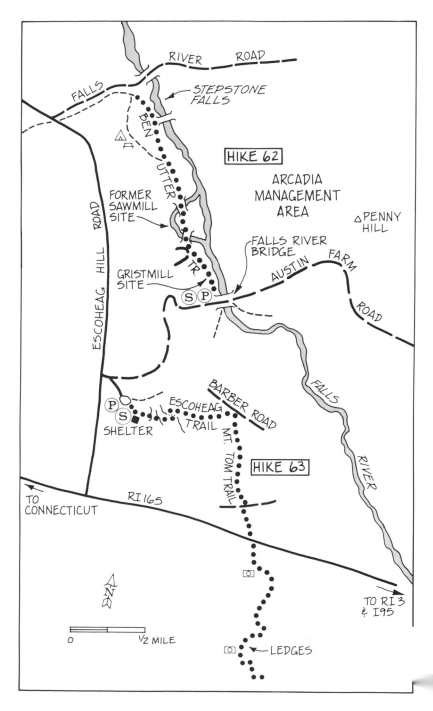

RIVER   ROAD

FALLS

STEPSTONE
FALLS

BEN   UTTER   TR.

HIKE 62

ARCADIA
MANAGEMENT
AREA

△PENNY
HILL

FORMER
SAWMILL
SITE

FALLS RIVER
BRIDGE

AUSTIN   FARM

ROAD

GRISTMILL
SITE

ESCOHEAG   HILL   ROAD

Ⓢ Ⓟ

BARBER   ROAD

Ⓟ
Ⓢ

ESCOHEAG
TRAIL

SHELTER

MT. TOM TRAIL

HIKE 63

FALLS

RIVER

TO
CONNECTICUT

RI 165

TO RI 3
& I95

N

0   ½ MILE

LEDGES

from this most appealing sight. A better idea is to begin at the bridge off Austin Farm Road. (Avoid hiking Arcadia in the late fall and winter because hunting is permitted then.)

From RI-165 in Exeter, take unmarked Escoheag Hill Road (1.8 miles east of the Connecticut–Rhode Island border and 5 miles west of the I-95 underpass). Travel north 0.9 mile and turn right onto the first gravel road, Austin Farm Road. Travel 1.8 miles east to Falls River Bridge. A sign posted on a pine tree on the west side of the river announces the start of the Ben Utter Trail. (Austin Farm Road may be closed from one side during certain times of the year, so you may have to walk the 1.8 miles to the bridge or begin at the falls. Another option is to take RI-165 to Frosty Hollow Road, about 4 miles east of the Connecticut border, which eventually intersects with Austin Farm Road. Turn left and drive about 3 miles to the Falls River Bridge.)

The yellow paint-blazed path follows the western bank of the river for the first 0.5 mile. After crossing a wooden bridge over a swampy section and passing the foundation of an old gristmill at 0.3 mile, the trail rises to a knoll overlooking the river and continues on a ridge above the water. Keep an eye on young children here. At close to 0.5 mile, the trail bears left away from the river and soon merges with a dirt road. Don't cross the road, but turn to the right and pick up the trail as it heads back into the woods. At 0.6 mile, impressive mountain laurel thickets swallow hikers for 100 yards. A bridge over a major tributary brings you to the remains of a sawmill and a small waterfall, visible across the stream on the left. The trail crosses back over the tributary toward higher ground and continues its course some distance from the river. At the 1-mile mark, the path becomes less easily traversed due to mud and fallen trees. Keep the kids moving by suggesting that they watch for the white-blazed trail back to the river's edge.

At 1.3 miles, pick up the white-blazed side trail (the yellow-blazed trail leads to a camping area with a shelter and fireplaces but no water). Though somewhat indistinct, the rocky path essentially follows along the river. Step onto the bridge at 1.6 miles for a good view of the rushing water and the cascades. The kids can play "Pooh sticks" (from one of the classic A. A. Milne Winnie-the-Pooh tales) by tossing sticks off one side of the bridge and quickly running to the other side to see whose stick will appear first. At 1.7 miles, you will reach Stepstone Falls and Falls River Road. Stop for a picnic lunch before heading back to the parking area on Austin Farm Road and your car.

63. Escoheag and Mount Tom Trails

Type: Dayhike
Difficulty: Moderate for children
Distance: 5.2 miles, round trip
Hiking time: 3 hours
High point/elevation gain: 435 feet, 420 feet
Hikable: April–early November
Maps: USGS Voluntown and Hope Valley

The Escoheag Trail to the Mount Tom Trail offers kids who love to scramble up and down rocky hills a number of places to climb, especially within the first mile. Children under five will need assistance with several rocky stream crossings in the initial leg of the trip. Younger ones will feel safe running ahead on the second mile of trail crossing Mount Tom ridge; it is well worn, extremely level, and straight. On the approach to the final cliffs of-

Stone shelter along the Escoheag Trail

fering fine views, the people-sized boulders, perched precariously on either side of the trail, will inspire kids to invent all sorts of trailside games. The Arcadia Management Area operates several campgrounds, the closest being the one off Escoheag Hill Road.

From RI-165 in Exeter take unmarked Escoheag Hill Road (1.8 miles east of the Connecticut–Rhode Island border and 5 miles west of the I-95 underpass). Travel north 0.9 mile and turn right onto the first gravel road, Austin Farm Road. After 100 feet, take another right onto a road that leads to a circular parking area in 0.1 mile. Look for the white-blazed trail at the southern end of the parking area.

Head at once down a rocky slope with conveniently placed log steps. Watch for a side trail at 0.1 mile (marked with a blue-and-red ribbon) that leads to an impressive stone shelter atop a massive outcropping. The views may be somewhat obstructed by foliage, but stopping at such an appealing point so early in the walk will interest children in what lies ahead. Back on the main trail, at 0.3 mile, a smooth rock plateau offers a potential picnic spot on the return trip. Several stream crossings test the kids' ability to select appropriate stepping stones. After crossing the largest of the brooks at 0.5 mile, the trail takes a sharp right turn. Soon, cliffs will appear on the left side of the trail.

Just short of 1 mile, Escoheag Trail meets a dirt road (Barber Road). Do not cross the road, but take a sharp right-hand turn back into the woods onto Mount Tom Trail (look for the trail and "no snowmobile" signs). For 1 mile as the trail travels the ridge, the path is very level (and somewhat soggy at first). Kids will enjoy the tunnel effect of the abundant mountain laurel bushes. Eight-tenths of a mile from the beginning of the Mount Tom Trail, the path meets a dirt road. Diagonally across the road on the right the trail continues in a southerly direction. At 1.1 miles,

Mount Tom Trail crosses RI-165 . Here, the kids should wait for you so that you can cross this highway together. Walk in an easterly direction across the highway to rejoin the trail (watch for the

sign). Two-tenths of a mile from the highway are cliffs with pretty western and southern views. While the adults enjoy the panoramas, the kids can try their hand at "rock climbing" on the trailside boulders. Continue for another 0.6 mile to the ledges of Mount Tom offering lovely views to the south and west. The dropoffs are steep, so keep an eye on the kids. Relax with a snack and then return to your car the way you came.

64. Pachaug Trail Around Beach Pond

Type: Dayhike
Difficulty: Difficult for children
Distance: 6.4 miles, round trip
Hiking time: 5 hours
High point/elevation gain: 440 feet, 340 feet
Hikable: April–November
Maps: USGS Voluntown

The blue-blazed Pachaug Trail, a woods trail that wanders for about 30 miles through southwestern Rhode Island into southeastern Connecticut, offers a combination of enticing features: water, views, rock formations, and forest. The portion of the trail that skirts Beach Pond is one of Rhode Island's most rewarding inland hikes, though also one of the most strenuous. While younger children will have difficulty navigating the rugged terrain, the older ones who are more experienced hikers will delight in the challenging scrambles as the trail winds around the lake. Near hike's end, they will find renewed energy in their search for the "lemon squeezer."

From Voluntown, Connecticut, drive east on RI-165 across the causeway that divides Beach Pond (just over the Connecticut border) to the parking area on the left.

Join the Pachaug Trail (traveling the same route as the yellow-blazed Tippecansett Trail) on the eastern end of the parking area as it skirts the beach and bath house. Follow the prolific blue-and-yellow blazes up an immediate ascent to a high bluff overlooking the pond. Within the first 0.1 mile, the trail swings toward the pond though it remains about 30 feet above the water; side trails afford good pond views. Soon the trail veers back into the woods, challenging hikers with the first steep climbs and descents. At 0.4 mile, the path bears diagonally left across a dirt road; 0.1 mile later, the Pachaug Trail leaves the Tippecansett Trail and heads northwest (left) on rolling terrain. The next half mile takes hikers to the water's edge at regular intervals via side trails. Kids will enjoy climbing the numerous large, flat rocks that border the path and jut out over the water. A swampy area

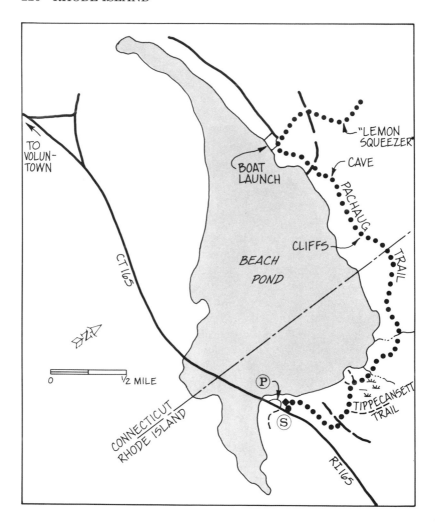

and stream crossings at 0.8 mile present a soggy challenge but soon the trail resumes its rolling, rocky character. Kids can look for fox or raccoon tracks—or otters themselves—in the area near the stream.

After a stream crossing at 1.3 miles, the trail turns away from the pond and does not offer water views for more than 1 mile. The trail crosses several active streams and follows under cool stands of hemlocks. Along this section of the trail, children can watch for indications (marked trees) that they have entered Connecticut. At 1.7 miles, younger hikers will need assistance traversing a steep cliff. For the next 0.3 mile, the numerous ups and downs with rock obstacles make for tough going. The trail follows one narrow ridge that is cut into a rock face 30 feet high. A bluff at 1.8 miles might make a pleasant spot for an energy break. Just before the 2-mile mark, the trail passes an Indian cave with a precarious rock overhang that will tempt children to enter; the ceiling seems close to collapse, however, so kids should admire the cave from several feet away. After a pleasant stretch in the woods, the trail crosses a dirt road at 2.2 miles. Soon after, the pond becomes visible again as the trail continues about 10 feet above the water.

You will reach the boat launch area after a strenuous 2.5-mile hike. (A second car can be left here if you don't wish to hike the return route. Follow the boat launch signs off of CT-165.) The trail picks up at the far end of the parking lot, close to the road, and continues north. After traveling along cliff's edge for 30 yards, the trail heads into the woods and crosses a woods road at 2.7 miles. At 2.8 miles, a steep drop into a gorge followed by a rocky ascent demands careful climbing and scrambling. Small children with a short stride will have to be carried in some places. The interesting rock formations and small caves will bring out the adventurous spirit in everyone. A double blue blaze at 2.9 miles indicates a right-hand turn. The trail clings to the base of cliffs towering 60 or 70 feet high. The first child to see the "lemon squeezer" (a tight passage between the side of a cliff and a long rock slab) wins. (Hint: it is along the cliff just to the right of the blue-blazed trail about 0.5 mile from the boat launch area.) It is important that children follow the path at stream's edge rather than try to maneuver along the cliff to the lemon squeezer. Continue to a set of smaller cliffs at 3.2 miles or turn around at the "lemon squeezer" and head back to your car the way you came.

65. Arcadia Trail

Type:	Dayhike
Difficulty:	Easy for children
Distance:	3 miles, round trip
Hiking time:	2 hours
High point/elevation gain:	466 feet, 320 feet
Hikable:	April–November
Maps:	USGS Hope Valley

Arcadia Trail in the Arcadia Management Area is maintained by the Rhode Island chapter of the AMC and is popular in the summer months with local folks as well as out-of-towners due

Mountain laurel in bloom

to the easy and interesting jaunt to the public beach and picnic area. (Even in the fall, though, you are bound to encounter fellow hikers.) Brook crossings, small ponds, and forest strolls will keep children enthused until it is time to dive into Browning Mill Pond. Camping is available within the Arcadia Management Area off Escoheag Hill and Frosty Hollow roads.

From the junction of RI-165 and RI-3 in Exeter, take RI-3 south for 1.5 miles to a large log structure on the right. (If you pass the sign that says "Entering Richmond," you've gone too far.) Park here and begin your hike at the southwest corner of the building.

The white-blazed trail is narrow but readily identifiable. It sweeps quickly north along noisy I-95, then merges with a wide dirt road, slips under the overpass for I-95, and meets a gate. Go through the gate into a camping area (now closed) and continue straight through the campground heading west on the road to a T intersection. Walk straight across the intersection and join the Arcadia Trail indicated by double yellow blazes. In the next 0.5 mile, several brook crossings demand careful stepping; the bridge traversing one swampy and rocky area (at about 0.8 mile) is in poor condition.

Just after you notice a small lily pond on the left at about 1 mile, a double yellow blaze indicates a right-hand turn. Instead of continuing on the Arcadia Trail, follow the white-blazed trail straight ahead. The trail turns right in 50 feet. At the right turn, a side trail accesses a small pond and affords good views of the water and a small cascade. Back on the trail, you will pass another small pond on your left. Soon you will reach part of the nature trail created in the mid-1970s by the Youth Conservation Corps. Signs identify common and not-so-common plants and trees. At 1.3 miles you reach paved Old Nooseneck Road. Straight across the road is Browning Mill Pond with picnic tables, pavilions, and a beach for swimming.

After the children have enjoyed a refreshing swim and picnic lunch, you can take the path to the western end of the pond and then reverse the directions to reach your car. (If your group feels particularly energetic, you can extend the hike by bearing left at the intersection with the yellow-blazed Arcadia Trail, where a right turn leads back to your car. This trail meanders through the woods for over 0.5 mile, crosses Old Nooseneck Road, parallels Bates Schoolhouse Road—a dirt road—and then turns right on this road in about 0.1 mile. The trail heads left through a road barricade onto a grassy, unused road as Bates Schoolhouse Road heads right and soon turns right at double blazes into the woods. The path continues on rolling terrain through the woods for 1 mile before ending at RI-165. By reversing the directions and returning to your car, you will have completed a 6.5-mile hike.)

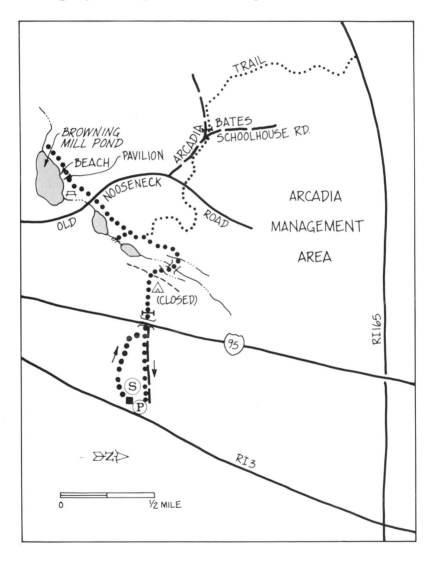

66. Long Pond

Type: Dayhike
Difficulty: Moderate for children
Distance: 2.4 miles, round trip
Hiking time: 2.5 hours
High point/elevation gain: 405 feet, 300 feet
Hikable: April–November
Maps: USGS Voluntown

This section of the Narragansett Trail, nestled in the countryside of western Rhode Island, winds through the 340-acre Long and Ell Ponds Natural Area and rates as one of the most enticing inland walks. Children and adults alike will marvel at Long Pond's distinctive grove of hemlock trees referred to as "The Cathedral," its granite cliffs towering 70 feet above the water, and its colony of giant rhododendron. (If you visit in July, the rhododendron plants will be in bloom.) A deep ravine joins Long to Ell Pond, a smaller lake surrounded by swamp and a quaking bog. Don't be misled by this hike's relatively short distance—rocky ascents and steep drops will have even the fittest children huffing and puffing. Kids should be encouraged to wear proper hiking boots, not slippery sneakers.

From the eastern junction of CT-138 (also called Spring Street in Rhode Island) and CT-165, drive 5.4 miles on CT/RI-138. Immediately after the turn for Camp Yawgoog, turn right onto Wincheck Pond Road in Hopkinton. Go 0.2 mile and turn right onto Canonchet Road; the post office will be on the left. After 0.4 mile, bear left at a fork (still on Canonchet Road) and drive 0.6 mile to a parking area on the right. If you're coming from the western junction of RI-3 and RI-138, travel 2.7 miles on RI-138, heading west, and bear left onto Wincheck Road. In 0.1 mile, turn left onto Canonchet Road and follow the above directions.

This trail, which will take you along the edge of the ridge rising from Long Pond, begins at the western corner of the parking lot. After a short woods walk, the path divides; take the yellow-blazed right-hand trail. The trail wanders through an area covered with mountain laurel, along a shallow, sloping ledge, then winds through a maze of boulders and trees rising over Long

Looking over Long Pond

Pond. At about 0.4 mile, you will come upon two huge glacial boulders. The larger one may remind kids of a ship's hull cutting through the water.

Frequently, as you travel about 35 feet above the water, you will see the cliffs or bluffs to your right across the narrow neck of Long Pond and also down at the eastern head of the pond. At 0.5 mile, the trail begins one of the numerous descents through a hemlock grove and then climbs back up to the height of the ridge. The yellow-blazed path follows along the ridge and descends through another shaded forest area strewn with rocks. This area, known as "The Cathedral," boasts hemlocks that are among the oldest in the state—some approach 200 years old. If you can find a tree stump, have children count the rings.

The trail continues its rugged ascents and descents, heading west, and at 0.8 mile tumbles down into the damp channel that joins the two ponds. Here, you will see the distinctive giant rhododendrons towering up to 16 feet. Crossing the sometimes swollen

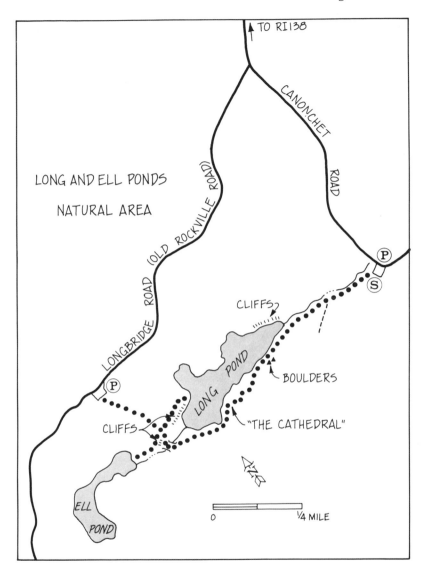

LONG AND ELL PONDS

NATURAL AREA

TO RI 138

CANONCHET ROAD

LONGBRIDGE ROAD (OLD ROCKVILLE ROAD)

CLIFFS?

LONG POND

BOULDERS

"THE CATHEDRAL"

CLIFFS

ELL POND

0   ¼ MILE

ravine on the log footbridge requires careful stepping and assistance for younger hikers. Although the trail out of the ravine is steep, strategically placed stones make ascending the 60 vertical feet to the top quite negotiable for children. A dramatic cliff wall dominates the left side of the trail. After scrambling out of the gorge, you'll come to a four-way trail intersection. Straight ahead, a northbound trail leads to a parking area on Longbridge Road. First, take the eastern and western side trails that lead to high cliffs with impressive views of Long and Ell ponds. Back at the trail intersection, continue to follow the footpath north to the reservation exit. On the way, you will descend another huge granite slab, pass under a second area of mighty rhododendrons, and walk along the edge of a 15-foot cliff before reaching the road. (Hold the hands of younger children along this stretch.) You can retrace your steps or, if the kids have had enough scrambling for one day, turn right onto Longbridge Road, walk 1 mile, and turn right onto Canonchet Road. Stroll 0.6 mile to your car parked on the right.

Notes: Camping and fires are prohibited. The area closes one-half hour after sunset and reopens one-half hour before sunrise.

67. Napatree Point

Type: Dayhike
Difficulty: Moderate for children
Distance: 3.5 miles, loop
Hiking time: 3.5 hours
High point/elevation gain: 30 feet, 30 feet
Hikable: Year-round
Maps: USGS Watch Hill and Mystic

What child wouldn't enjoy a walk along a sandy beach to the ruins of a turn-of-the-century fort? Napatree Point, a long, narrow peninsula that juts into the sea at the southwestern tip of the state, was the site of Fort Ninigret. Dismantled in the1930s, the fort exists now only as cellar holes and crumbling platforms. With the fort as a destination, kids will be inspired to keep moving, although the soft sand makes for tough going and the constant sun (there is no shade) saps energy quickly. This barren peninsula has been repeatedly assaulted by storms rolling in off of the ocean. The hurricane of 1938, in addition to destroying the summer cottages that once cluttered the point, changed the shape of the land, turning Sandy Point, the northern tip, into an island.

Skirting the dunes at Napatree Point

You can introduce the kids to the hobby of bird-watching here since the point offers hikers choice seats from which to observe the fall hawk migration (especially in late September). Also watch for osprey, merlin, and cormorants.

Take Exit 1 off of I-95 and head southwest on RI-3. In 4 miles, turn left and head south on RI-78 for another 4 miles. Turn left (south) onto RI-1A. In Avondale, turn right (southwest) onto Watch Hill Road. Follow this road to Watch Hill Center. Park on the main road in a metered space. (Parking is limited so arrive early in the morning or hike on a weekday or off-season.)

The trail begins near the yacht club, at the far right (western) corner of a parking lot for local residents visiting Napatree Beach. Head left over the sand dunes to the water's edge on the peninsula's left side. In the distance, you can see the knoll at the tip of Napatree Point, site of the fort ruins. The hike takes you to the fort and back along water's edge, with no marked or distinct trail once you have reached the sandy beach. Bring buckets and shovels for scooping sand and collecting shells and smooth stones. After following along the shore for about 1.7 miles, you will reach the fort ruins, which are not appropriate for climbing and are somewhat dangerous. It is probably a good idea to arrive here together rather than allowing the kids to rush ahead.

Return via the northern side of the peninsula along Fishers Island Sound. Ask the kids if they notice a difference between the bay and ocean sides. On a blustery spring or fall day, the dunes separating the two bodies of water provide welcome refuge from the relentless ocean winds. The sea birds, too, appreciate a respite from the breeze and strut along the water's edge and congregate on sand bars in the bay. (Give the kids the binoculars for an up-close look at the birds.) From this side of Napatree Point, you can get a good look at the nests often occupied by osprey. After a total hike of about 3.5 miles, you will reach Watch Hill center, where you parked your car.

68. Ninigret Beach

Type:	Dayhike or overnight
Difficulty:	Moderate for children
Distance:	5 miles, round trip
Hiking time:	3.5 hours
High point/elevation gain:	10 feet, 10 feet
Hikable:	Year-round
Maps:	USGS Quonochontaug

In the spring bring a kite, in the summer a bathing suit and towel, and in the fall take along a book to identify seashells, especially if you opt to camp here and anticipate having some time on your hands. This two-mile-long beach lies between the Atlantic Ocean and Ninigret Pond, a popular spot for clamming, in the Ninigret Conservation Area. As with most ocean walks, there are no paths to follow, just the water's edge, so children can lead the hike just as well as the parents. Although it may seem that without trail intersections, stream crossings, or rocky scrambles, a hike such as this might get monotonous, the ocean never ceases to fascinate younger folks. They thrill to the sheer expanse of water and to the roaring, rolling waves that continuously deposit tiny treasures in the sand for collecting or tossing back into the foamy water. In the summertime, the parking lot (which accommodates fewer than 100 vehicles for a fee in-season) often fills quickly so arrive early or hike in the off-season.

Take East Beach Road off of US 1 in Charlestown, just east of the RI-216 intersection. This road leads to the parking area for the beach that is sandwiched between Ninigret Pond and the Atlantic Ocean.

Head south from the parking area along a sandy strip to the ocean's edge. Gaze eastward up the beach to the distant boulders guarding the Charlestown Breachway, your destination. With little but windswept sand between you and these rock soldiers, they seem much closer than 2.5 miles away. Hugging the water's edge for easier walking, hike down the beach, pausing often for the kids to poke in the sand for seashells and stones buffed and polished by the relentless waves. At 0.5 mile and again at 1.5 miles, you will pass camping areas on the left. Once you have

Horses and riders on Ninigret Beach

walked beyond these populated spots, the crowds thin and you share the beach with sea gulls rather than sunbathers. At the breachway, approximately 2.5 miles from the start, spread out the picnic lunch while the kids scramble up and down the large rocks. Explore the edge of Ninigret Pond on the return trip if you wish, equipped with binoculars for bird-watching, and eventually return as you came along the beach.

69. Fort Barton/Sin and Flesh Brook

Type: Dayhike
Difficulty: Easy for children
Distance: 2.8 miles, round trip
Hiking time: 2 hours
High point/elevation gain: 100 feet, 80 feet
Hikable: Year-round
Maps: USGS Fall River

From atop the observation tower at the site of Fort Barton on the Smith Rock Trail, kids will not have a hard time imagining themselves as Revolutionary War soldiers scanning the harbor for British ships. Although nothing resembling a fort remains at this site, the park is dotted with boulders and mounds for climbing. (The earthworks that have survived are intentionally unrestored.) The trail from the fort site winds back and forth across the river like one strand in a braid; some of these frequent river crossings have rather rickety bridges, though one Tiverton resident assured us that the bridges will be replaced soon. Children will need the help of an adult to manage these river crossings as they currently are.

From the junction of RI-24 and RI-77 in Tiverton, take RI-77 south to Lawton Avenue, following a sign for Fort Barton. Travel on this street 0.3 mile to an intersection with Highland Road. On the right side of Lawton Avenue is the Tiverton Town Hall and across the intersection is a cliff with a large sign for Fort Barton. Parking is off of Highland Road, across from the town hall.

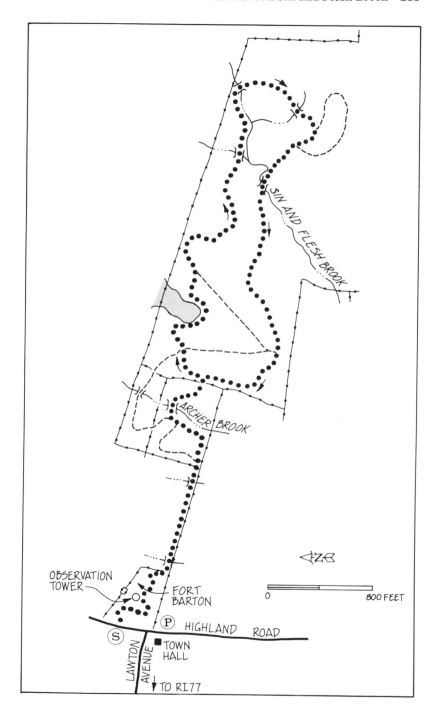

SIN AND FLESH BROOK

ARCHER BROOK

N

0   800 FEET

OBSERVATION
TOWER

FORT
BARTON

P   HIGHLAND   ROAD

S

LAWTON
AVENUE

TOWN
HALL

TO RI 77

Negotiating the log steps at Fort Barton

You reach the fort by walking along Highland Road for 100 feet or so from the parking area to a paved road with a chain across it. This road climbs quickly, winding around to an observation tower that provides remarkable views of the narrow strait where patriots once feared the logical crossing of British soldiers trying to capture more American territory. Give the kids a little history lesson to enhance their appreciation of this historic spot.

The main trail through Fort Barton Woods, which begins behind the fort site on a gravel path, is marked with red arrows. (The blue trails are secondary paths leading to points of natural interest such as unusual patches of mushrooms or wildflowers.) Heading southeast, the trail descends quickly by way of a steep and rugged set of stairs through a nature area where various species of plants and trees are noted with wooden tags. With a fence on the left and a stone wall on the right, continue straight ahead, on the red-blazed trail, crossing two bridges. (Appoint one of the kids to keep track of the bridges; the total count should be seven.) Cross Archer Brook on the third bridge and follow the red trail through a stone wall. Just beyond that point, the red trail splits, indicated by signs on a towering red oak. This hike, primarily heading east and west, is a terrific opportunity for a young hiker to practice compass reading skills. Ask him or her to keep track of your direction and give frequent updates.

Follow the left-hand path, initially traveling north. (You will loop around and emerge from the right-hand side.) Heading generally east, skirt the edge of a pond and cross Sin and Flesh Brook over a fourth bridge about 1.2 miles from the start. Then cross three more times within the next 0.5 mile. The kids will have a delightful time exploring the riverbank. The river and the path wind around one another, making for an interesting walk and somewhat treacherous stream crossings. (Instruct kids who run ahead to wait for adult help at bridges.) Return to the fort site by following the red arrows in a westerly direction to the initial split in the red trail at the oak tree. Here bear left to retrace the first 0.4 mile of the hike and return to your car.

70. Cliff Walk

Type: Dayhike
Difficulty: Moderate for children
Distance: 6 miles, round trip
Hiking time: 3 hours
High point/elevation gain: 40 feet, 40 feet
Hikable: Year-round
Maps: USGS Newport

While the adults are gazing at the mansions—the sixty- or seventy-room "summer cottages"—that line one side of this path, the kids will no doubt be looking in the other direction—at the sea crashing against the rocky shoreline, the surfers skimming precariously atop the waves, or the boats bobbing far from shore.

Midway along the famed Cliff Walk with Land's End in the distance

Much of this route, especially during the early part of the hike, is easy to navigate with a stroller. On most occasions when the path rises high above the sea, sturdy fences will prevent accidents but there are spots where the path skirts precipitous cliffs and younger children will need to be watched. Don't come to Newport expecting a solitary hike; this is one of the state's most popular attractions, especially during the summer months.

From the east or west, drive into Newport via RI-138. Turn south on RI-138A and drive 2 miles to Memorial Boulevard. Turn right and you will soon come upon Easton Beach (also called Newport Beach) on the left, where there is parking for "Cliff Walkers." During the summer there is a fee for parking here. A drive down Bellevue Boulevard followed by a left down any number of side streets will bring your further into the hike with less crowded parking conditions. If you are traveling in two vehicles, you may want to park your second car at the other end of the trail on Ocean Avenue (reached by driving down Bellevue Avenue and turning right at street's end).

The hike begins behind a restaurant named Cliff Walk Manor on what is essentially a sidewalk. In less than one mile, you will reach Forty Steps, a stairway leading to the rocks at water's edge. On the right, just past the steps, you will have your first unobstructed views of the mansions, some of which are part of the Salve Regina College complex. Here, late nineteenth-century architecture contrasts with modern dormitories and other contemporary buildings. Just beyond the college is The Breakers, summer home of Cornelius Vanderbilt. This mansion, as well as Rosecliff, Marble House, and others, is open to the public for a fee. At 1.7 miles, Rosecliff, where *The Great Gatsby* was filmed, is shielded from view behind a massive wall.

If the kids are getting bored with the ocean scenery, play hiking bingo: See who will be the first to spot a sailboat, a surfer, a fisherman, a seagull. Count dogs, people wearing hats, babies in strollers, or people sporting sunglasses. Or take turns verbally designing your own dream oceanfront mansions. (Notice the vast difference in descriptions between the preschooler and the preteen, or the preteen and the parent!) After traveling through two tunnels and passing Marble House, the trail becomes rockier and heads for the southern tip of the peninsula called Land's End. Here the cliffs plunge 25 feet to the water. Kids will need assistance on some tricky ascents as you pass more palatial estates. After a three-mile walk, you will reach Land's End, also the name of the last mansion along the Cliff Walk. As you round the tip of land, you will have magnificent views of Rhode Island Sound. The trail ends on Ocean Avenue. Locate your second car or hike back along the shore to the parking area at Easton Beach.

71. Norman Bird Sanctuary

Type:	Dayhike
Difficulty:	Moderate for children
Distance:	3 miles, round trip
Hiking time:	2.25 hours
High point/elevation gain:	70 feet, 120 feet
Hikable:	Year-round
Maps:	USGS Prudence Island and Newport

Although many folks come to this 450-acre property with binoculars and bird-watching guidebooks, others come—several thousand each year—to visit Hanging Rock. Whether its name derives from the unusual configuration of this hunk of pudding stone or the legend that criminals were once hung there is not known. You can be sure, however, that your children will not soon forget scaling the steep, bumpy cliff wall and traveling along the ridge to Hanging Rock with spectacular views over the ocean, marshes, and Gardiner Pond. By the very nature of the sanctuary's diverse terrain, the hike divides itself into two parts: the initial route takes you over wide, grassy paths through rather tame territory, whereas the second half of the walk on narrow, rugged wooded trails to Hanging Rock adds spice to what would have been a rather sedate outing by kid standards. As you travel all of the sanctuary paths, you'll wish you had brought a tape recorder rather than your camera to record the visit. Despite the number of birds you see, you will hear even more. And for some reason, once you've left it's harder to remember the lovely sounds of this place than the sights.

 From RI-138A in Middletown, turn east onto Green End Avenue. At the corner of Green End Avenue and Third Beach Road (a four-way intersection), take a right onto Third Beach Road. (A

Dramatic ocean views from Hanging Rock

sign on a telephone pole indicates the way to Norman Bird Sanctuary.) Drive 0.7 mile to the sanctuary and park near the sanctuary buildings.

Begin your walk on the path that heads north from the headquarters, parallel to Third Beach Road. Join the Old Fire Road, bearing right, at 0.3 mile and turn right again at 0.5 mile to join the Forest Ridge Trail, a former bridle path. Remain on the Forest Ridge Trail for 1.2 miles, staying right at two intersections with the Woodcock Trail. Bear right at the Red Maple Swamp Pond and in 300 feet bear left and left again to a junction with the Hanging Rock Trail 1.4 miles from the start. Follow this trail (which runs along Hanging Rock Road) for another 0.2 mile before reaching the pudding rock cliff that is your destination. Climb up, letting the kids go first so that you can follow closely behind. They'll love the feeling of being genuine rock climbers as they choose solid footholds and inch up the rock face. Follow the rock ledges to the left for magnificent ocean views from Hanging Rock. To either side, the rock drops away to valleys far below. Rest here before making a tricky descent to the wooded trail (kids will need assistance with the climb down) and returning to the intersection with the Forest Ridge Trail.

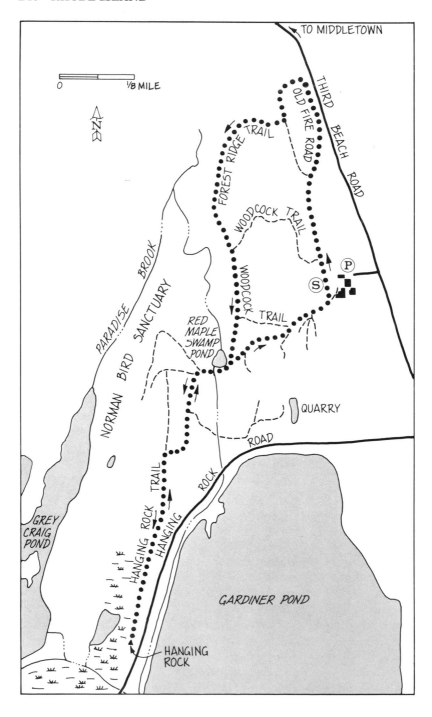

TO MIDDLETOWN

0   ⅛ MILE

N

THIRD BEACH ROAD

OLD FIRE ROAD

FOREST RIDGE TRAIL

WOODCOCK TRAIL

WOODCOCK TRAIL

P

S

PARADISE BROOK

NORMAN BIRD SANCTUARY

RED MAPLE SWAMP POND

QUARRY

ROAD

HANGING ROCK TRAIL

HANGING ROCK

GREY CRAIG POND

GARDINER POND

HANGING ROCK

Bear right for a northeasterly route back to the sanctuary headquarters (where there are rest rooms). If you visit in March, you may witness woodcocks engaged in their strange and noisy mating ritual along this last section of trail; the first woodcock courtship of each year is celebrated by sanctuary staff with fake champagne as a sign that spring has arrived. Before you leave, take time to visit the injured animals—usually birds, but sometimes raccoons or skunks—in the cages near the main building. They are released as soon as they have recovered.

Notes: There is a small admission charge for persons over age 11. A trail map is available at the headquarters. Picnic in the designated area near the barn. No pets are allowed on the trails. The sanctuary is open year-round, seven days a week, from 9:00 a.m. to 5:00 p.m. Gate closes at five.

72. Rodman's Hollow

Type: Dayhike
Difficulty: Moderate for children
Distance: 4.3 miles, loop
Hiking time: 3 hours
High point/elevation gain: 70 feet, 100 feet
Hikable: Year-round
Maps: USGS Block Island

Sitting just 12 miles off the Rhode Island coast, Block Island has been popular as a summer retreat for 100 years. The island is accessible year-round by ferry, and for kids this is sure to be one of the trip's most memorable events. The ferry ride from Point Judith takes about an hour. Currently, cars cost over $40 round trip and there is a charge of $10 (same day round trip) for each person 12 and older. (You can rent mopeds and bicycles on the island if you prefer to leave your car on the mainland.) You should make a reservation by calling (401) 783-4613 (*months* in advance if you plan to take your car across during the summer). Since camping on the island is forbidden, you may want to arrive early in the day and leave on the evening ferry or stay overnight in one of the hotels or guest houses. Rodman's Hollow, one of several popular hiking areas, is a 37-acre wildlife refuge with several different trails that offer visitors a good look at the variety of plant and animal life on the island.

From New Shoreham center, drive south on Pilot Hill Road to a right turn onto Mohegan Trail. Drive about 1 mile to another right-hand turn onto Lakeside Drive. In another mile, turn left

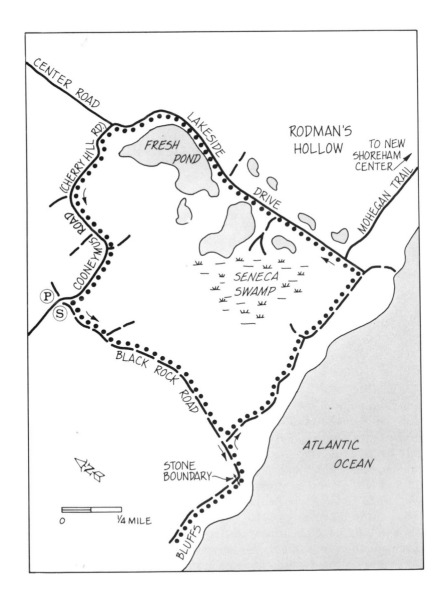

onto Cooneymus Road (called Cherry Hill Road on some maps). Drive 0.7 mile and park on the right side of the road across from the Rodman's Hollow sign.

Begin on the rutted jeep trail (Black Rock Road) near the Rodman's Hollow sign. At 0.3 mile, a jeep trail splits off to the left; continue straight on the main trail. In another 0.5 mile, a dirt road bears left while you continue straight on a less traveled road. At 1 mile from the start, the road ends, marked by a stone boundary to prevent vehicle access. Continue ahead on the path to the bluffs, which are quite high above the ocean and should be approached with caution. Children who venter down side trails to bluff's edge should be accompanied by an adult. Travel along these magnificent bluffs, watching the patterns created by the ocean's incessant attacks and retreats. Turn around at the top of the bluffs. (For a shorter hike, return the way you came.) To continue, turn left at the rock barricade and right within 0.1 mile, bearing right at all subsequent forks to stay close to the ocean and arriving at an intersection with Mohegan Trail 1 mile from the bluffs. Turn left onto this road and immediately join Lakeside Drive. Follow Lakeside Drive for 1 mile past Seneca Swamp and a series of small ponds to a left-hand turn onto Cooneymus Road and a 0.7-mile walk to your car.

73. Block Island National Wildlife Refuge

Type: Dayhike
Difficulty: Easy for children
Distance: 1.5 miles, round trip
Hiking time: 2 hours
High point/elevation gain: 5 feet, 10 feet
Hikable: Year-round
Maps: USGS Block Island

A sandy beach road stretching along the dunes of Block Island's northernmost tip is the major trail within and adjacent to the 29-acre Block Island National Wildlife Refuge. In addition to the always fascinating sights and sounds of the ocean, this hike includes two points of historical interest: Settler's Rock, where the island's original inhabitants landed with their cattle in April 1661, and the North Lighthouse, the fourth lighthouse on this point, built in 1867. Kids will be amazed at the number of sea-gulls here: This is a primary nesting area for these ocean birds and thousands make the refuge their summer home.

 From New Shoreham center on Block Island, drive north on Corn Neck Road to its conclusion (about 4 miles). Park in the Settler's Rock parking area at road's end.

The monument erected near Settler's Rock marks the begin-ning of the hike along the beach road. As you walk past Sachem

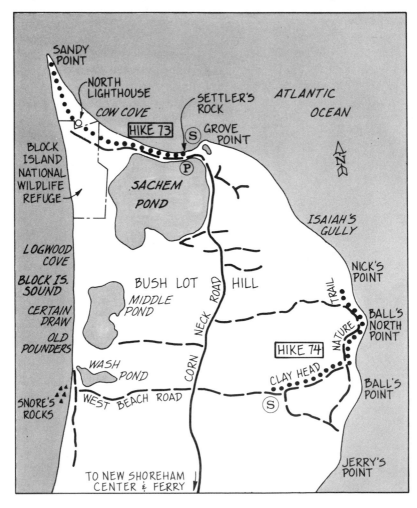

Pond, skirting the sand dunes, children should be reminded to stay on the road to avoid disturbing the seagull nesting areas because protective parent gulls may attack intruders. Although you may be fortunate enough to catch a glimpse of a seagull chick, it is difficult to spot the fluffy, grayish-brown birds because they blend in so well with the beach sand.

Continue walking along the edge of Cow Cove, scanning the sand for pieces of driftwood, stiffened seaweed, or bits of shells. After about 0.5 mile, you will reach North Lighthouse, which is soon to be renovated and turned into a maritime museum. Sandy Point, which extends further north into Block Island Sound, is a sand spit that continues to expand (several feet each year) as the sediments from the eroding cliffs of Clay Head and Mohegan Bluff are continuously washed ashore here. Take time to explore, then return to Settler's Rock the way you came.

North Lighthouse through the mist

74. Clayhead Nature Trail

Type: Dayhike
Difficulty: Easy for children
Distance: 2 miles, round trip
Hiking time: 2 hours
High point/elevation gain: 100 feet, 180 feet
Hikable: Year-round
Maps: USGS Block Island

Hiking the trails at Clay Head will appeal to anyone who appreciates ocean bluffs, beachcombing and bird-watching. The cliffs known as Clay Head tower 50 to 100 feet over the pounding surf and stretch 2 miles along the northeastern side of the island. If you visit in the fall (especially late September or early October), you will witness flocks of birds stopping here during the peak of migration. More than 100 different species may be present at any time, giving even bird-watching novices a chance to spot a rare variety. Look for barn owls, yellow-throated warblers, and peregrine falcons.

 From New Shoreham center, drive north on Corn Neck Road 3.3 miles and turn right (east) onto a dirt road (unmarked but with a wooden post that says "Clayhead Trail"). Drive to a small parking area off the road 0.3 mile from Corn Neck Road at a second sign.

The trail at the head of the parking area, well marked with arrows on wooden stakes, winds through a salt marsh (Clayhead Swamp) and travels over a short boardwalk. On the right, you will notice an interesting contrast as a peaceful, hilly pasture separates you from the formidable ocean. In about 0.3 mile, you will reach the beach. Admire the cliffs of Clay Head to your left, composed of sand and the multicolored clay for which this area is noted. These cliffs are your destination.

This rocky beach is a good place for kids to collect sea treasures as well as a good spot to stop for a snack on the return trip. Avoid a multitude of side trails heading left (west); stay to the right on the Blue Stone Trail. The path leads over a grassy area to the top of the bluffs where the view of the surging waves is just as

Bold seagull

impressive. Follow the Clay Head Trail as it travels north-to-south along the upper edge of the bluffs and eventually tapers off and ends, 1.5 miles from the start. Here, you reverse direction and head back to your car. Clay Head's 11-mile trail system with numerous, unmarked side trails crisscrossing the rolling expanse of low vegetation is sometimes referred to as "the maze." Keep landmarks well in mind if you leave the north-south trail on the bluff's edge.

75. Mohegan Bluffs

Type: Dayhike
Difficulty: Moderate for children
Distance: 4 miles, round trip
Hiking time: 3 hours
High point/elevation gain: 200 feet, 400 feet
Hikable: Year-round
Maps: USGS Block Island

The breathtaking cliffs that constitute Mohegan Bluffs rise to 200 feet above the ocean, distinctly marking nearly five miles of Block Island's coastline. It is hard to imagine the child who wouldn't stand in awe of the mighty cliffs, strong and steadfast against the battering of relentless waves and the mighty winds rolling in off the ocean. Visitors might be surprised to find out that, according to geologists, the bluffs are eroding at a rate of about 5 feet each year. If you opt to descend the cliff wall to the shore, children will need a hand. Another highlight within the 26-acre overlook is the Southeast Lighthouse, built in 1874. This historic building can be seen by ships 35 miles away.

No driving is necessary; exit the ferry landing near New Shoreham center. (See hike 74 for details on the ferry.)

The hike begins at the ferry port. Walk east down Water Street to Ballard's Beach and 0.4 mile along the shore (in a southerly direction) to Pebbly Beach. Soon, South East Light Road swings close to the water's edge. Take this road left (south) as it gradually ascends for the next mile until you reach the entrance to Mohegan Bluffs and the Southeast Lighthouse on the left, 1.5 miles from the start. Head to the lighthouse and then follow the steep footpath to the base of the cliffs. Children will need assistance on this stretch. Here, explore the beach to the left and right. As you wander, the kids can look for driftwood and shells, pretty rocks, and interesting tracks in the sand.

Eventually retrace your steps and climb back to the top of the cliffs at the lighthouse. Return to South East Light Road and turn left. Walk just over 200 yards to an automobile turnaround on the left side of the road. Here, a hiking trail leaves the turnaround southward and travels along the top of the bluffs to the east. As you hike along the edge of these awesome cliffs, look out over Corn Cove, Sheffield's Cove, and the Fishing Rocks. Can the kids understand why folks long ago thought the world was flat? When the trail ends, return to the ferry the way you came.

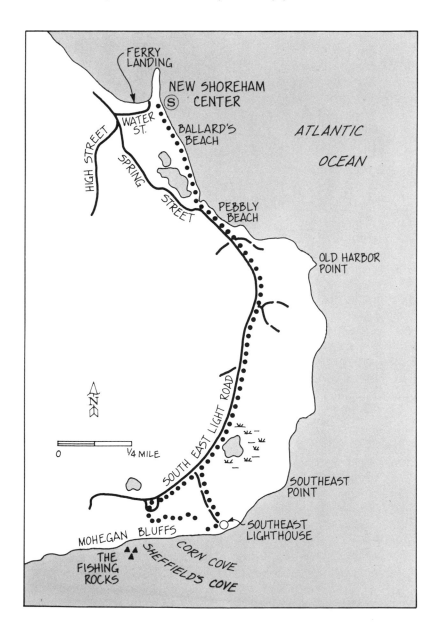

Useful Addresses

GENERAL

The Appalachian Mountain Club
5 Joy Street
Boston, MA 02108
Publishes much hiking-related
material, including the *AMC
Massachusetts and Rhode
Island Trail Guide*

Distribution Branch
U.S. Geological Survey
Box 25286, Federal Center,
Building 41
Denver, CO 80225
Distributes USGS maps

New England Orienteering Club
9 Cannon Road
Woburn, MA 01801
Publishes detailed New England
maps

New England Trail Conference
33 Knollwood Drive
East Longmeadow, MA 01028
Publishes map of New England
hiking trails and reports on
trail and shelter conditions

Walking News, Inc.
P.O. Box 352
Canal Street Station
New York, NY 10013
Publishes map covering the
South Taconic area of
Massachusetts, Connecticut,
and New York

CONNECTICUT

Connecticut Audubon Society
93 West Cornwall Road
Sharon, CT 06069

Connecticut Forest and Parks
Association
16 Meriden Road
Route 66, Middlefield
Middletown, CT 06457
Publishes the *Connecticut Walk
Book*, a guide to the major
hiking trails in Connecticut

The Nature Conservancy
Connecticut Chapter
55 High Street
Middletown, CT 06457
Owns and manages over 8,000
acres in Connecticut

State of Connecticut
Department of Environmental
Protection
Office of State Parks and
Recreation
165 Capitol Avenue
Hartford, CT 06106
Provides upon request a
comprehensive brochure on
state parks and forests as well
as detailed information with
maps on backpack camping in
Connecticut

State of Connecticut, Economic
Development
(Tourism Information)
865 Brook Street
Rocky Hill, CT 06067

MASSACHUSETTS

Friends of Quabbin, Inc.
Quabbin Visitor Center
Box 485
Belchertown Road
Belchertown, MA 01007

The Massachusetts Audubon
    Society
South Great Road
Lincoln, MA 01773

Massachusetts Department of
    Environmental Management
Division of Forests and Parks
100 Cambridge Street, 19th Floor
Boston, MA 02202
Will send on request a detailed
    brochure of Massachusetts
    forests and parks, including
    related camping information

Massachusetts Office of Travel and
    Tourism
100 Cambridge Street
Boston, MA 02202

New England Cartographics
P.O. Box 369
Amherst, MA 01004
Publishes color maps of areas in
    western Massachusetts

The Trustees of Reservations
572 Essex Street
Beverly, MA 01915
Custodians of seventy properties
    across Massachusetts

Williams Outing Club
SUB Box
Williams College
Williamstown, MA 01267
Publishes hiking guide with maps
    covering the Williamstown
    area and Greylock
    Reservation

RHODE ISLAND

Rhode Island Audubon Society
Powder Mill Ledges Wildlife
    Refuge
12 Sanderson Road
Smithfield, RI 02917

Rhode Island Department of
    Environmental Management
Information Office
9 Hayes Street
Providence, RI 02908

Rhode Island Tourism Division
Department of Economic
    Development
7 Jackson Walkway
Providence, RI 02903
Will send on request a camping
    guide describing state,
    municipal, and privately
    owned campgrounds

INDEX

CYNTHIA AND THOMAS LEWIS are residents of East Sullivan, New Hampshire. Cynthia is a full-time mother and author of several books, including *Mother's First Year*. Tom is an envi-

ronmental chemist. Avid outdoorspeople, they have explored every corner of New England together on a tandem bicycle. After the arrival of their two children, ages four and two, the Lewises continued their explorations on foot.

THE MOUNTAINEERS, founded in 1906, is a non-profit outdoor activity and conservation club, whose mission is "to explore, study, preserve and enjoy the natural beauty of the outdoors . . . " Based in Seattle, Washington, the club is now the third largest such organization in the United States, with 15,000 members and four branches throughout Washington State.

The Mountaineers sponsors both classes and year-round outdoor activities in the Pacific Northwest, which include hiking, mountain climbing, ski-touring, snowshoeing, bicycling, camping, kayaking and canoeing, nature study, sailing, and adventure travel. The club's conservation division supports environmental causes through educational activities, sponsoring legislation, and presenting informational programs. All club activities are led by skilled, experienced volunteers, who are dedicated to promoting safe and responsible enjoyment and preservation of the outdoors.

If you would like to participate in these organized outdoor activities or the club's programs, consider a membership in The Mountaineers. For information and an application, write or call The Mountaineers, Club Headquarters, 300 Third Avenue West, Seattle, Washington 98119; (206) 284-6310.

The Mountaineers Books, an active, non-profit publishing program of the club, produces guidebooks, instructional texts, historical works, natural history guides, and works on environmental conservation. All books produced by The Mountaineers are aimed at fulfilling the club's mission.

Call or send for catalog of more than 300 outdoor books published by:
The Mountaineers
1001 S.W. Klickitat Way, Suite 201
Seattle WA 98134
1-800-553-4453